# PAUL BABY

# PAUL BABY

☆ ☆ ☆ ☆ ☆ ☆ ☆ ☆ ☆ ☆

## Confessions
## of the
## Mayor of
## Kneesville

## by PAUL DIXON

### Introduction by Bob Hope

THE WORLD PUBLISHING COMPANY
Cleveland and New York

Published by The World Publishing Company
2231 West 110th Street, Cleveland, Ohio 44102
Published simultaneously in Canada by
Nelson, Foster & Scott Ltd.

*First Printing 1968*

Designed by Christine Wilkinson
Library of Congress Catalog Card Number: 68–29836

Printed in the United States of America

To

*Marge, Pam, and Greg*

with love

# Contents

# Illustrations

# Introduction

*by Bob Hope*

☆ So Paul Baby is writing a book! That's the kind of news that shakes you up. I understand that when the news got out, three teenagers in Kokomo burned their library cards.

But that Dixon is quite a guy. They call him the Mayor of Kneesville, which is a city you won't find on any map. It's in the heart of a bunch of fine ladies. I'm proud to say the Mayor of Kneesville is my friend. But he's stingy. He won't give me the keys to his city. He's keeping all those knees to himself.

In an introduction you're supposed to say nice things about the book or its author. That's hard to do where Paul is concerned. He cheats at golf. Against him Arnold Palmer and I don't stand a chance. Each time we putt, he mentions John Murphy's name—and that's all she wrote. How can you putt with one hand over your heart?

I thought Paul was kidding at first—about John Murphy's name, I mean. But it's true, ladies. Whenever Murphy's name is mentioned around WLW-Television, everyone puts his hand over his heart.

*11*

They've got one secretary who must be all heart. You should see where she put *her* hand!

What a crazy—and what a wonderful—place WLW-Television is. I first met that bunch when I was in Cincinnati raising loot for Judge Benjamin Schwartz's Hope House. Thanks to them we had ourselves a real whingding during the Bob Hope Benefit Golf Match. And we raised the cash we needed to modernize that 150-year-old building which houses those deserving boys. But we still need cash, so keep those dimes and dollars coming in. Right, Judge Schwartz?

So much for the commercial. Now back to that place called WLW-Television in Cincinnati. They do *live* television there. Not taped. Not filmed. But live. Doesn't that grab you? Hours and hours a day of it, too. Maybe that Murphy didn't get the word that "live" television went out with Bing Crosby's button shoes. Or maybe that Murphy is a wise old owl who knows something we don't. All I know is, that Irishman has the Midwest sewed up tighter than a drum with his live television. Kiddie shows and my old movies don't stand a Chinaman's chance against performers like Dixon. As the ladies say:

"Only a woman knows what another woman wants at five o'clock in the morning."

On the Dixon show they say *nine* instead of *five* but I'm writing this on the West Coast and there's a time difference. I may not be good, you see, but I'm neat. Sitting out here I know I'll get the best lines. When I was a guest on Paul's show, do you know who got the best lines? The prop boy. But I can't complain. They allowed me to move the props.

Actually the prop boy didn't have the best lines. The best lines belonged to those girls: Colleen Sharp, Bonnie Lou, and Marian Spelman. That Colleen— what a great talent. Paul says they put rocks in her pocket so she won't blow away. She's *that* tiny. If she does blow away, I hope there's a strong west wind. I'll be out on my roof with a net. And that Bonnie Lou! She is the only girl I know who can ad lib a Swiss yodel that turns out to be a commercial for coffee. And Marian. Now there's a singer for you. Real patriotic, too. When I walked down the street with her, every time she passed the American flag, she sang the National Anthem—all the way through! It took us two hours to go one block.

I don't see how Paul Baby gets away with what he does: he is the star of the show but he lets every-body else be top banana. How generous can a guy get? But that's Paul. He's generous to a fault—and one of the faults on his show once was me. When I made the mistake of asking for a script, he handed me a package of wieners, a fruit cake from Xenia, and a pair of binoculars!

And that Bruce Brownfield Band! The greatest, simply the greatest. You should hear them play "On, Wisconsin." They play it all the time. They have to. It's the only number they know. They play it every time they turn around on the Dixon Show, which is dangerous to do. Never turn around on the Dixon Show. He has more ad libbers in the audience than the Gabors have diamonds. Turn your back on Dixon's audience and—presto! some nice lady from Muncie has taken over the show and is slaying them with one-liners about hippies.

Only kidding, Paul. And I know you know it. Only kidding, Mr. Murphy. See. I've my hand over my heart. Personally I think one of the nicest things ever to happen to television in the Midwest has been the combination of John Murphy behind the scenes and Paul Baby out there in front. And your viewing area is lucky to have a guy like Dixon who is as nice off the camera as he is on.

And that is more than I will say for the prop boy. He wouldn't let me keep the wieners.

But good luck with your book, Paul. Jack Benny promised to buy a copy—once it comes out in paperback. Now that's what I call an endorsement. The last time Jack Benny bought a book, books were a novelty because Gutenberg had just invented movable type!

Cordially,

*Bob Hope*

# PAUL BABY

# 1.

# Paul Baby

☆ They laughed when I sat down to *talk* a book.

But, lady, everybody knows that I'm not a writer, I'm a talker.

So each night I come down here to my room in the basement and talk into a dictating machine. The next morning I take the dictation to the office where Alma Overholser gives me a strange look but types it up anyway. This has been going on for a long time now.

"What kind of book will it be?" one of the ladies in the studio audience asked me. "Will it be funny?"

"I think so," I said. "At least when I told Marge [that's my wife] I was writing a book, she started to laugh. That's some indication, isn't it?"

On the other hand, it might be no indication at all.

Ever since I told Marge that I was writing this book, she has been in high spirits. Whenever she looks at me she begins to laugh all over again.

When my daughter Pam heard about my book, she didn't say a word. She just sighed. Hasn't said a word to me since—and that's been months now. I guess Pam is afraid that "old blabbermouth" will "tell all" in the book just as he tells all on the show.

My son Greg reacted differently. When he heard I was writing the book, he asked for an increase in his allowance. But what has that to do with a book? Nothing, I suppose. He's always asking for an increase in his allowance. For instance, I can walk into the dining room and say: "Well, I think it might rain tonight."

"Does that mean I'll get an increase in my allowance?" Greg will say.

Only kidding, lady! About my family's reaction to this book, I mean. They wouldn't treat the old man that way. So this gives you an idea of what kind of book this will be: dumb in some places, silly in others, and—now and then—awfully serious. Because writing —or talking—a book is new to me, be kind and forgive my errors, will you? I make a lot of mistakes on the show, don't I? Why should I do any better when I'm doing a book?

Writing a book without putting my foot in my mouth simply would not be the Dixon we know!

So what *kind* of book will this be? Well, first off, I ain't important enough to write the story of my life. Let's get that fact squared away here and now. But, as I say on the show each morning, a lot of you are interested in what goes on *behind* the scenes of the

Dixon Show and television in general. You are interested in what the performers are *really* like. You should hear the questions you women in the studio audience ask me every day when our show is over. I figure if the studio audience keeps asking the same things over and over, *you* might be wondering, too. So that is what this book will do: answer the questions you women keep asking me.

You women run my show; you might as well run my book, too!

For instance, one question is how on earth did I get the name "Paul Baby." Well, the phrase didn't originate with me, because nothing on the show originates with me. I just arrive at the studio each morning and let the show happen. The phrase "Paul Baby" originated with one of our prop boys, Al Bischoff, now a leading salesman with the Drackett Company. It's amazing how our prop boys have gone upward and onward to big things in the world. Most of them, when they are prop boys such as Scratchy, are students at the University of Cincinnati or Xavier University. The irregular hours of their class schedules coincide with the irregular hours here at Avco Broadcasting, but none of this explains how I got the name "Paul Baby," does it? And you thought this book was going to be organized!

Well, lady, a few years back I bellowed for the prop boy to bring me something from off camera. Al Bischoff handed it to me, leaned over, patted me on the head, and said cheerfully: "Okay, Paul *Baby!*"

And that was how *that* got started. The name has stuck with me ever since. I could never get rid of it, even if I wanted to.

Where did the expression "Mercy!" originate? A lady in the studio audience started us saying that.

So you see who writes our shows: you women—plus the station personnel and anyone else—including delivery men—who happens by at the time. You all come up with much better stuff than we could, even if we had dozens of writers. So the success of the Dixon Show belongs to you. We're there, each morning, but you women make the show happen.

And look at the monster you created! When our show first played the Ohio State Fair in Columbus a few years back you caught us by complete surprise. We thought no one in his right mind would be there at nine in the morning so we scheduled our show from the WLW-Television Building which held only 300 people. Were we ever wrong!

You started to arrive at six that morning—and by nine, *mercy!* there was a line that was blocks long! Now we do our show from the Grandstand to over 50,000 people during fair week. And what do we *do*? The same dumb stuff day after day. So why do people watch? Darned if I know!

All I know is that a friend of mine (I won't give his name but his initials are Larry Knollman) was home recuperating from an operation. Having nothing else to do, he tuned us in. According to his wife Carol, one morning he began shouting: "Come here, Carol! Carol! Quick!"

She dashed in thinking he was in pain, but there he was, pointing at my dumb face on the tube, and he was saying: "Watch now, Carol. Watch! Here's what Paul is going to do next. And this is what he will say . . ."

And sure enough, I did and said exactly what he said I would.

Carol told me later: "Paul, I gave Larry a funny look and said, 'Larry, you're an intelligent man. You've a good education. And you're nobody's fool. But if you *know* what Paul is going to do and if you *know* what Paul is going to say, why are you watching him?' Paul, he shook his head. He said he didn't know. He said he guessed he was hooked!"

Another lady viewer moved back into the area after five years' absence. She turned our show on—and found us still doing the same old stuff. Our show hadn't changed in five years. But did she quit watching? No. She said she was hooked!

But how can we do the same show every day, five days a week, year after year, hang onto our old viewers and—according to all the rating services—keep attracting new ones? The secret is: we do the same show every day but we don't do the same show every day. Clear as mud, isn't it? Well, I'll try to explain it later on in the book, lady. I mean, there must be some way to explain why our show receives over 150,000 pieces of mail a year, most of them addressed to "Paul Baby." We don't hang onto you viewers just because we give away that big Oscherwitz salami every morning, although we have passed out nearly 3,000 salamis so far and—as they say about miniskirts—the end is still not in sight.

Also our show isn't successful just because it plays to the natives of Ohio, Indiana, Kentucky, and Illinois. Consider the outsiders—the newcomers—we win over. Read this letter a lady wrote from North Carolina:

"All the years I'd lived in North Carolina I heard about how much smarter you people in the north were. So a year ago we moved to Cincinnati. And in our motel room while waiting for our belongings to arrive, we turned on the television set. And what was on? You! You'll never know the feeling I had that morning. I asked my husband, 'Honey, what kind of area is this for us to raise our children?' By that time I decided that all the intelligent people just had to be back in North Carolina. But you know after watching your dumb show a few times I'm hooked? Your show is now the highlight of my day. Only a woman knows what another woman wants at nine o'clock in the morning! They want the same dumb thing: *you!* But don't tell my husband I wrote this because, Paul Baby, he still thinks you're dumb. Only during the Thanksgiving holidays he watched your show, the same one you always do, and he said, 'Well, it's not quite as bad as it used to be, is it? That Dixon has improved.'"

Perry Como never gets mail like that!

The average age group of our audience? We have a lot of senior citizens who think young because they take Upjohn Unicap Seniors, but the majority of our audience is between the ages of eighteen and forty-nine, with the greatest percentage being between the ages of twenty and thirty-five. And out of that 150 who visit us at the studio each day, at least one is on the nest! No wonder we sell Gerber Baby Food and Pampers—as well as Upjohn Unicap Seniors! Everyone seems hooked but the babies.

And where did that expression—"I'm hooked!"—come from? Well, when our show first went into Indianapolis where not a soul knew us, I used to tell viewers there: "You watch two or three weeks and I'm warning you: you'll be hooked!"

How *well* did we hook them? In our first year on the tube there we hooked 47 per cent of the local viewing audience! And when we gave out the salami award up there, nearly 600 people lined the streets just to see us visit Pat Slipcea in her home!

*Mercy!*

So that gives you an idea of the show which is on the tube each morning from 9:00 to 10:30 A.M. in Cincinnati, Dayton, Columbus, and Indianapolis; and community antennas scattered beyond the reach of those basic television areas. And that will also give you an idea of this book, which will try to answer questions about that show. The book will tackle big things and little things, big things like the talent that the three girls of our show—Bonnie, Colleen, and Marian—possess; and little things, like do I wear makeup on camera? Nope, lady. Only a little powder on my nose—because it's red.

This book will tell you about my movie career. I'll bet you didn't know I had one, did you? And this book will tell about my career in the theater. I'll bet you didn't know I had a career *there*, either, did you? Oh, this book will tell all kinds of personal stuff, some about me, but most about the people who make the Dixon Show the success that it is.

For instance, this book will answer the question that the Internal Revenue Service is always asking: "Is Bonnie Lou actually as rich as you say?" After all, there is more to Bonnie than meets the eye, but what meets the eye ain't bad, either. She and I have the same birthday: October 27. You knew that, didn't you! Then why didn't you send us a card or present last year? Try to do better this year, will you?

The point is, you women in the studio audience are forever asking me, "What is Bonnie Lou really like?" Well, I have a whole chapter devoted to that wonderful yodeler. Bonnie has told me things that she has never even told her husband Milt. She made me promise never to breathe a word of that stuff to anyone. I have included every last thing she told me in this book. That's the kind of blabbermouth *I* am!

You will meet the serious side of Bonnie Lou as well as the Bonnie Lou who can light up a room, because that is the kind of book this is, too. We're a close-knit family on the Dixon Show, we've had our moments of tragedy, and we've shared those lonely behind-the-scenes moments together—as a family should. Now, with your permission, we'll share those moments with you—via this book—because you're a part of the Dixon Show family, too, aren't you?

You women are always asking *how* I got into broadcasting. We'll go into that and prove that while I have no talent now, I had even less at the beginning of my career. That doesn't sound right but you know what I mean. What I mean is, when I was a boy I used to walk the streets of Albia, Iowa, talking to myself and pretending I was the world's greatest radio announcer. Also, back then, I was in love with Betty Fairfield, Jack Armstrong's girl friend on the radio program. I include intimate stuff like that because sex helps sell books. I'll tell all about my radio childhood.

You'll find Bruce Brownfield and his band in the book, too. Did you know that Ruth Lyons knew Bruce when Bruce was in kneepants? If you did, lady, you cheated: you started this book from the *back*—and that ain't fair. We'll discover things about Bruce Brownfield that even his barber never found out, like how Bruce wants his hair combed after a haircut— "Wet or dry?"

The reason Bruce and his musicians are in the book is the same reason Bonnie, Colleen, Marian, and the rest are: they are as much a part of the Dixon Show as I am. They give out more autographs than *I* do! *That* should tell you something but if you find out what, lady, keep it to yourself because I would rather not know. I have enough trouble keeping ahead of the game as it is. Maybe when I'm older I'll know better. Right now I'm exactly thirty-eight years old. Isn't that right, Bruce?

You women are always asking me why I keep telling Bruce to shut up. This book tells why.

Another question I'm asked a lot is, "Are remote telecasts hard to do?" Those are telecasts which we do from other cities. Hard to do? For Gordy our producer, yes. For me, no. All I have to do is show up— and worry. Gordy, whose full name is Gordon Waltz, and his crew take care of everything. They are the *real* professionals. Want to know how to organize a motorcade? Gordy and his crew can tell you. In fact, after you've read the chapter on Gordy and the remote telecasts, you'll know as much about remotes as I do.

"Your commercials seem painless. Why don't other announcers do commercials that way?"

That's another question you in the studio audience ask me. So we'll answer that one in the book, too; and I have the funny feeling that when our sponsors read the answer we might not have any sponsors left!

Our show is hard for me to explain, isn't it? You watch the show every day and you can't explain it, either. Think of trying to explain it sight unseen! That's the headache the WLW-Television salesmen have when they visit advertisers in parts of the country where our show is not on the tube. How they do it—or try—is also another behind-the-scenes glimpse we'll give you in this book.

As we say, there are a lot of behinds in television— and as a viewer, you have a right to know them better. Speaking of such things, Frank Pierce, the weatherman on the Dixon Show, got into the act, too, when he announced: "A big new front is moving in, followed closely by a big behind!"

Only on the Dixon Show could you get a weather forecast like that!

You ladies write in to ask what happens when you finally arrive at the studio to be part of our studio audience. We'll tell that, too, so that you at home still waiting to visit—tickets are out two years in advance! —will know what to expect. You'll learn things like what the studio looks like, how handsome I am, and other interesting things which—now that I think about them—aren't *that* interesting at all!

And you keep asking me what I do when the show is over, implying that I hurry right off to the mission. In a later chapter you'll spend a full day with me— from the time I get up to the time I hit the sack. Visit clients with me. Take an evening stroll with me—and with Greg's dog Pepper. Ride with me along Columbia Parkway to and from work. Oh, I'm not moaning

that I work myself to death, but can I suggest that
there's more to the Dixon Show than meets the eye?
Spend a day with me and see what I mean.

"Paul Baby, were you *really* a radio disc jockey?"

I'm asked that by newcomers to the area and by
those of you who were Uncle Al prospects in the days
when there was no Uncle Al in Cincinnati. Yep. I was a
radio disc jockey; and I'll tell you all about it.

Some women ask me how I feel television today
compares with television in the early days when
nearly every program was "live." The women wonder
if things have changed much. So we'll look at those
early days of television or at least the part of them
I know about. But fair warning: this book won't be
any text that can be used in a history course; *my*
recollections have to do with things like an elephant
that wasn't housebroken.

Actually, you'd be surprised at some of the stuff
that went on when television was young. But don't
frown, lady. Those days ain't gone forever. Each
morning the Dixon Show is the same as it was back
then—*live*. The only difference is, now we make mistakes in living color. When our faces are red, you can
tell!

Then there's John Murphy. *Hand over your heart,
lady!* If some of you think he's a character I invented,
let me correct that impression fast. After all, he signs
the checks that Marge cashes. John Murphy, our fearless Avco Broadcasting President, is actually responsible for the Dixon Show being on the air in the first
place. I realize that when I say it that way some of
his friends will never speak to him again, but he did
put me on the air so the fault is as much his as mine.

Somehow that doesn't sound right, either, but you know what I mean.

What I'm saying is, John does have a few faults, the biggest being that he looks upon St. Patrick's Day as a national holiday and complains each year because the post offices remain open. John, who is—I believe—somewhat Irish, drives a green car, and writes thousands of memos a day—in green ink. Avco Broadcasting is flooded with these Murphy memos which we all call "greenies." Only this morning Rosemary Kelly met me in the hall and said generously: "I'll trade six of my greenies for three of yours."

After I write the chapter on John Murphy I might not have a job at the station, but that's the way we writers are. I'll call the shots as I see them and let the greenies fall where they may. Besides, John Murphy can't fire me. I've hidden his green ink.

This book will tell you also what the real Bob Braun is like—or at least, I think it will. How can you write about a guy who does pushups? But did you know that he and I worked together at WCPO-TV? You did? Well, lady, pretend you didn't and act surprised when you read it later on in this book. Did you know that I paid for the first record Bob Braun ever made? And that I first met Bob Braun when I was master of ceremonies of a Harris Rosedale amateur show? Lady, if you know so much, you should have written the book! Mercy!

Well, then, I'll tell you things about Vivienne Della Chiesa that will astound, amaze, and confound you. At the moment I can't think of what those things will be because I haven't written that chapter yet, but I can't wait to read that one myself. And I'll tell you how Nick Clooney is when he is not on camera. And the way Rosemary Kelly is. And Ruby Wright. Listen, lady, I may tell so many real inside things that the rest of the Avco personnel may never let me near the studio again.

How did Colleen Sharp get the nickname Tink? Is her husband Mike really an Indian—and will there be an Indian uprising? I intend to write about these things. I'm writing about Marian Spelman, too. Do her high notes shatter glass? Can a high-class singer from Corryville find true happiness on a farm that has one lamb, one horse, and Bill Nimmo? As you can see, this book will leave no stone unturned. Heavens, it actually frightens *me* to think of the repercussions after you have read this book and have discovered what really goes on! Well, we must be brave. I'll write the book and tell all—about everybody else but me. How's that for being brave?

Ruth Lyons? Will she be in this book? Lady, you bet your boots she will be. That wonderful lady made WLW-Television what it is today. You're darned right she'll be in this book. Everything will be in this book!

So, having set the stage and established that this book is going to be a mixed-up mess the same as the Dixon Show is, let us turn the book over to the women and try to answer their questions. As John Murphy says: "Paul, you should be great at answering questions. Of all the talent we have at Avco, yours is the most questionable."

On that friendly note, lady, shall we begin?

*First* question, please . . .

# 2.

## *Paul Baby &*

# RADIO

☆ "Paul Baby, were you *really* a radio disc jockey?"

You'd better believe it, lady. And to make matters worse, I was once a radio newscaster! How do you like them apples!

So when I brag sometimes about how good radio was "in the good old days," you can see that it wasn't as great as memory paints it.

Mary Wood wrote in the *Cincinnati Post & Times-Star:* "If it helps, Paul, you were a better disc jockey than you were a newscaster."

And she was right as rain. I was a better disc jockey than I was a newscaster. Why? Well, Mary explains it herself. She also wrote: "Paul, you were the world's *worst* newscaster!"

She didn't hurt my feelings when she wrote that. I agreed with her completely: I *was* the world's worst newscaster, so anything else I did had to be better. I am a better dancer than I was a newscaster—and I can't dance a lick. I'm a better singer than I was a newscaster; and you've heard me sing. The really nice thing—and the only nice thing—about being the world's worst newscaster is that whatever else I did, I just had to be better than that.

See how cheerful I am? I keep looking for the silver lining! Haven't found it yet, but it doesn't hurt to look, does it? What I mean is, I certainly can't go back and get my old job as a newscaster. That's what I really mean.

But what kind of disc jockey was I? I can sum that up in three words—

*Corny, corny, corny!*

And, as you beautiful residents of Kneesville well know, I haven't changed too much since then, have I? Still, I don't think I could qualify as a disc jockey these days. Today's disc jockeys are a different breed because radio itself has changed. When *I* was a disc jockey, WLW-Radio's Richard King had yet to invent any illnesses. But he was winning fame as a standby announcer for the Yellow Cab Company.

Then he went into commercial radio—and was never heard from again.

Seriously, there were moments in my career when I thought I would never be heard from again. *Again* is the wrong word to use. A lot of times I thought I would never be heard from at all.

Example: when the first station auditioned me for a job as radio announcer, the program director suggested that I go back to my father's drugstore and work there.

"You've a great future ahead of you, kid," he muttered. "But not in broadcasting."

He also predicted that Dewey would defeat Truman; and when one of his announcers—"Dutch" Reagan— wanted to head on to greater things than broadcasting sports in Iowa, the program director probably told him: "You've a great future ahead of you, kid, but not in public life."

I wonder if he *did* say that to the governor of California? Oh well. . . .

The point is, lady, that although my career in radio got its shaky start in Iowa, it did not start rolling until I was hired by WAAF in Chicago. Now there was Big Time! Can you imagine me—old blabbermouth— as a sophisticated Chicago disc jockey? Chicago had trouble imagining it, too, so don't feel bad if you can't. Actually my career didn't start rolling in the Windy City, either. It did, however, pick up enough steam to keep the dream alive. As Chicago's "Sunrise Serenader," I didn't exactly take Chicago by storm. Chicago has more radio stations than Richard King has pills. When *I* was on WAAF, everybody listened to all the other stations. I can't even say that fame was fleeting. Fame? I had none.

And I had no big fat paycheck, either. To supplement our income Marge worked at Marshall Field by day, and when evening came she created casseroles. Marge could parlay one pound of hamburger into so many dinners that I didn't realize for several months that she was using hamburger at all. I thought we were on a meatless diet.

We lived in a small, dark, and airless apartment filled with second-hand furniture and silver trays we

had acquired at our wedding. Compared to the rest
of the tenants in that building we were at the bottom
of the economic heap. I think we were the first de-
pressed area the building had. Even the janitor made
more money than Marge and I did combined. Also, he
wasn't impressed that I was a radio announcer. I'm
certain of this because he kept asking: "Kid, exactly
what did you say you did?"

"I'm a radio announcer."

"One of them, huh?"

"Yes," I would say.

He'd shake his head and look at me with gloom.
Then he would say: "Kid, have you thought of getting
yourself a nice job at the post office? That's civil service and the pay is good, too."

I didn't take his advice but later on Marge did. Now,
every Christmas she drives her red, white, and blue
Thunderbird to the post office where she helps out the
season's rush by working as a sorter. By Christmas
Eve Marge is completely out of *sorts*. Get it? *Sorter* at
the post office. Out of *sorts*. Say, that's pretty good.
I must remember to use that on the show this Christmas. Where was I, though? Oh yes. I was telling you
about my "career."

Incidentally, speaking of starting out in the business
and of our morning show, now and then young men
fresh from broadcasting schools will watch the Dixon
Show from the studio audience. I can see in their
eyes the same stars I had—and still have—in mine.
And sure as shooting, after the show one of them
will say: "Mr. Dixon, what you do is *easy*. Why, I
could do your show with one hand tied behind my
back!"

If they expect an argument from me they're wrong, because they don't get one. I agree with them. And I'm not kidding, either. They are probably right. And what's more, they could probably do the Dixon Show better than I do. I mean this. But the trouble is, they want to start halfway up the ladder. I've had lean days but, corny or not, I stuck with the dream. These kids want their dreams handed to them on a silver platter. They don't want to eat a thousand casseroles to get here. Sure our show is easy to do. I don't say it isn't. But it took me a long time to get here, which is why I'm grateful. I didn't get here, wherever *that* is, by myself. Marge and a thousand others have shown me the way.

Do the show with one hand tied behind me? Why should I? I like the way I do it now: with one foot in my mouth!

Speaking of my foot in my mouth, I *did* have one brief moment of fame as a Chicago radio announcer. That was when the Garfield Park Lions Club let me— of all people—be the master of ceremonies in their show. It played, according to the advertisements, in the "beautiful million-dollar Paradise Ballroom; convenient to el trains, streetcars, buses, and with ample parking for autos . . . " Why did the club let me be master of ceremonies? Because one morning on the radio I opened my mouth and put my foot in it, that's why.

I casually suggested to whatever few listeners I had that WAAF should throw a little party so the listeners could see what us announcers looked like. When 3,000 letters flooded the station, mercy! You should have seen the station manager's face!

"A party for three thousand people?" he groaned. "Dixon, are you trying to bankrupt us?"

He did have a point. The station then had neither the money nor the room for a shindig for 3,000 people. What I mean is, if the station *had* had lots of money, it could have afforded to hire good announcers instead of corny creatures like me, fresh from the country. So the next morning I told the listeners of the problem I had: 3,000 people coming to a party—and no place to have it.

"My wife would love to have you all over," I said, "but I'm not sure how many of you can fit into our apartment. Besides, the janitor thinks I work at the post office."

Well, *that* was when the Garfield Park Lions Club came to the rescue. The club sold tickets for a dollar apiece—and the party was on again. I still have one of their handbills which describes the event:

CORN GALORE!

*Come and Get It All*
*With Paul Dixon!*

RADIO'S SUNRISE SERENADER
*In Person!*

*SIX FULL HOURS OF ENTERTAINMENT!*

GIGANTIC FUN FEST!

AD LIB JOKES & HOURS
OF SIDE-SPLITTING FUN & DANCING!

To make certain that people did turn out by the streetcarful, the Garfield Park Lions Club also brought

in Bert Wilson and Bill Anson, well-known Chicago
personalities of the hour. Who was the band that
played for the side-splitting dance filled with ad lib
jokes? Jimmy Jackson—and his Musical Men of Note.
The vocalists were Jane Carroll and Alan DeWitt.

Happily, the party was a success. Even sophisticated Chicago likes its share of corn.

Shortly after that grand event, Mort Watters of
WCPO-Radio was driving to Chicago, heard me make
a mess of my morning show, and decided that I was
just the voice he needed as a newscaster on his Cincinnati radio station. Well, where I'm concerned,
that's how station managers are. Whenever one heard
me on the air he assumed two things: (1) I was
about to be fired and (2) I must sure work cheap with
the kind of announcing I did. In fact, after I went to
work for WCPO-Radio I received a letter from a St.
Louis radio station manager who wrote in part:

". . . While on a visit to Cincinnati recently, I listened to several of your newscasts. I was quite impressed with your style and voice quality. It occurred
to me that you might be interested soon in making
a change and . . ."

Lucky for me I stuck with Mort!

In any event, Marge and I got established in Cincinnati. The roof of our car leaked and our furniture
sagged, so you couldn't exactly call our entry trium-
phant. We looked as if we were looking for a crop to
pick.

What was radio like then in Cincinnati? Well,
Bulldog Drummond was everybody's favorite on
WCPO-Radio and so was Tom Mix. Big deal! I inter-
viewed Tom Mix on Fountain Square! Jean Shepherd

was announcer at WSAI. Dick Bray was doing his "Fans in the Stands" program, Waite Hoyt was broadcasting the baseball games, and Paul Hodges could be found on the concourse of the Cincinnati Union Terminal, where he muttered "Arriving or leaving?" at the passengers who appeared on his "Train Time" program.

The first year in Cincinnati introduced me as a newscaster to one of Cincinnati's famous floods. I'll never forget that cold and dreary morning when I stood on the Eighth Street viaduct and described the flood breaking over the Mill Creek barrier.

Another news broadcast I'll not forget was from Fountain Square on V-E Day. I did a broadcast from there every forty-five minutes all day long—and until midnight! What a happy madhouse that old square was! People splashing around in the fountain and total strangers kissing and hugging. The celebration seemed to go on and on—and I was grateful to be one small part of it.

But the broadcast that is burned forever in my memory is the one that still gives me the shakes to think about. It happened in March, 1947. As news editor I usually worked from noon to six in the evening, but that day schedules went out the window. At nine on the morning of March 11, a six-story building at Pearl and Race streets collapsed. A half-dozen employees managed to scramble to freedom, but another half-dozen men were still trapped beneath the rubble. By noon, two trapped men had been freed. Jack Fogarty, Paul Hodges, and I were at the scene from noon on, doing direct radio coverage live.

One of the big things that stands out in my mind

is the heroism of the firemen and policemen. Those brave, brave men worked hour after hour, risking their own lives every minute of those hours, trying to reach the remaining trapped men. By eight that evening workers caught the faint cry of voices from deep within the rubble and—without hesitation—the rescuers dug a precarious tunnel underneath the rubble to where they thought the trapped men were. Assistant Fire Chief David Kuhn himself squeezed through that creaking tunnel to where the voices of the trapped had come from. And later, a microphone in my hand, I crawled through that same tunnel. Scared? You bet. Any moment the litter above us could have shifted and buried us, too.

"That was a great broadcast," a listener told me later.

Well, perhaps it was, but, I'll clue you, lady, I wasn't thinking of fame then. I was shivering in my boots. The radio listeners could hear the creak and groan of the structure that threatened to tumble down on us. And before I entered the tunnel, the microphone caught the words of Fire Chief Barney Houston, telling me that I entered at my own risk. I don't think I'll ever be as frightened as that evening when I entered that shaky and narrow little world. But God was good to me. He got me safely out again. And He allowed me to hold the microphone that picked up the faint voice of one of the men: Delmar Rudd, then eighteen years old, who had been in the wreckage since that morning. He wouldn't be brought out—alive—until twenty-four hours had passed.

When I got home the next morning, Marge bawled me out for taking chances, but all the time she was bawling me out, she had tears in her eyes. She was glad I was home again and safe. And so was I.

I don't ever want to go through that again—but if the need and the moment should arise? Well, I know I'd do it all over again . . . and without hesitation. What fame did I get from those historic broadcasts? In June, 1947, I was voted in a local poll as Cincinnati's top newscaster. How about *that!*

With the WCPO microphone, I recorded in sound another traumatic experience that broke the heart of Cincinnati. From Pittsburgh I broadcasted the death of Cincinnati's beloved riverboat, *The Island Queen,* that huge and wonderful vessel that had carried generations from Cincinnati upstream to Coney Island. But in Pittsburgh for an overhaul, the grand old side-wheeler exploded and burned to the water's edge.

It was at this time I first met Ed Schott, then president of Coney Island. Ed and I were to have many happy and busy summers at his amusement park, doing Paul Dixon television shows from Moonlight Garden. Now Ed is dead, may God rest his soul, and in Ed's place is Ralph Wachs, Coney's new president. He's still keeping the park's fine tradition and improving on it by adding new rides and features. I have a fond place in my heart for Coney Island. It was at Coney that I met so many of you personally.

But back to my days as a newscaster. Even when I was doing the news, I wanted in my heart to be a disc jockey. No matter how exciting broadcasting the news was and despite winning the award, I knew I wasn't really a good newscaster. Basically, I'm a cheerful guy—or is *corny* the word I want? And as Mary Wood once wrote: "When reporting the news

on the air, Paul, one should not sound *too* cheerful.
There's something wrong when you hear a cheerful
man describe an automobile crash!"

But I couldn't help it. That's the way I happened
to sound. I certainly wasn't cheered by death on the
highway. I'm sure you understand that, lady. So I
got lucky again. In addition to doing the news I was
allowed to do what I wanted to do right along: spin
records!

In 1951 *Coronet* magazine named me one of the
top ten disc jockeys in the country. But I must have
been lucky there, too. Offhand I could have named
a hundred disc jockeys who, that year, were head and
shoulders above me. Still, more luck was coming my
way. In 1948, Nick Kenny wrote in his nationally syndicated column: "Cincinnati, Ohio!!! Paul Dixon, your
disc jockey of WCPO, is really putting Cincinnati on
the map as far as Tin Pan Alley is concerned. The
New York music boys regard Dixon as one of the most
important platter spinners in the business."

Well, whether I was *that* important, I can't say.
All I know about those sunny days were the dinners
Marge cooked. She had switched from casseroles to
straight hamburger. We were, at last, coming up in
the world—a little.

As for corn, my brand of corn was heard whenever
you turned on WCPO-Radio back then. I did an interview program called "Breakfast at the Netherland"
where I interviewed women in the hotel coffeeshop.
Then came the "1230" Club—you'll never guess the
station's frequency in a million years!—every day
from 9:30 in the morning until 11:30; and I'd be back
each afternoon at 3:00 for two more hours!

What kind of a record show would I run? Not like the kind they run these days. I'd be lost. Now any record that stays on top for three days is called a golden oldie! No, I would clutter up the airwaves with records that I hoped appealed to everyone—teenagers as well as Mom. As the result, New York record makers began to look for my reaction before they would release a record nationally. They didn't consider me a brain at picking winners; they figured me for an ordinary guy and I guess it was easier for them to try new records on me first. Some claim that I personally made national hits of many records, pointing out "Underneath the Arches" as an example, but I can't see that. I'm flattered but it just ain't so. What I mean is, who am I to force anything off on you? Nobody can get the public to go for something that isn't good. The public turns up its nose fast at guys who think they can fool the women. No, in the record business I was just lucky enough now and then to be able to spot a winner—usually after everyone else had said so!

My days back then were long and involved. I would be on the air two hours in the morning and two more hours in the afternoon. On Saturday night I would do still another show called "Yours for the Asking." Also, each day I did a man-on-the-street program at 12:45—and when I had free time on Saturdays I was the master of ceremonies of a program called "Stars of Tomorrow," an amateur show. You'll never guess who showed up one day to be on that one—Bob Braun! Or if you read the first chapter, you didn't have to guess; you knew!

"We worry about you," one of the engineers said

back then. "Every time you get near a microphone, even if it isn't hooked up, you shout, 'Hi, Mom!' and do a commercial!"

He was right, too. I had to be careful walking downtown. Suppose I passed a radio store that had a window full of microphones? I would have launched into a commercial right there on the sidewalk! And someone would have hauled me away to the funny farm. I was like the vaudeville ham who went into his act whenever the refrigerator light came on.

Were the audiences back then good to me? Lady, you'd better believe it. They were better than I deserved—and that's the truth!

Consider what happened to my world August 14, 1948. Pam was born in Good Samaritan Hospital and frankly, it's a good thing John Murphy (*hand over your heart, lady!*) wasn't president of that hospital's lay committee then. When Pam was born, things sort of fell apart—in a most happy way—as reported by Harry Heskamp, editor of the *Mt. Lookout Observer:*

"The gentle-faced Sisters of Charity who operate Good Samaritan Hospital and who are noted for their calm and poise were a bit flabbergasted on and after August 14 when the radio fans reacted to the announcement that a girl had been born to Mrs. Paul Dixon, Delta Avenue, Mt. Lookout. If you wanted to be funny you might stretch a point and say they were 'rattled' after the 114th rattle had been delivered to Mrs. Dixon. In fact they were compelled to throw up their hands long before the mailman had delivered the 918th gift to the hospital. . . ."

See what I mean when I say people are wonderful! Pam received gifts of nighties, kimonos, robes, bottles, toy animals, and—by the hundreds—safety pins.

What frosted the cake for me and made me realize how truly great is the heart of this Midwest was when a couple of ladies walked into the *Cincinnati Post* newsroom where I did my newscasts and presented me with a savings account book made out in my new daughter's name. The book contained ten dollars. The ladies refused to give their names. All they would say was that the gift was from ". . . the ladies of your man-on-the-street broadcast every Tuesday!"

Later, in radio, Pam got into the act again, but this was when she was a little older and when WCPO-Radio had built a studio for me in the basement of our home because with my schedule I had been meeting myself coming and going. Pam would toddle into the home studio when I was on the air, climb on my lap, yammer into the microphone, and—with equal abruptness—say: "That's all!"

She would toddle away and not another peep could anyone get out of her. Pam—and later Greg—grew up with Cincinnati looking out for—and loving—them, too. Well, my two kids couldn't have had nicer godparents than the people who were kind enough to listen to me.

That was radio, but came the day there was a brand new thing called television. I took a dim view of television insofar as my abilities were concerned.

"What could I do on television?" I said once to Marge. "I'm a radio disc jockey. I can't sing. I can't dance. I can't even rollerskate. If I went into television, I'd end up flat on my face."

Marge just looked at me and grinned.

And didn't say a word.

I think she knew something I didn't.

# 3.

## *Paul Baby &*

## HIS RADIO CHILDHOOD

☆ "What about your childhood?" a woman in the audience today asked me. "Did you have any?"

Well, yes. And since I'm only thirty-eight, my childhood is easy to recall. You might label it a radio childhood because even back then I was hooked on broadcasting. I was also hooked on Betty Fairfield, who was the girl friend of Jack Armstrong. I was also hooked on chewing gum (still am!), kite flying, basketball bouncing, tree climbing, ice cream eating, and creek wading.

Mostly, though, I was hooked on radio. Incidentally,

the first announcement I ever made over an actual radio station was: "At the sound of the gong, it will be exactly 9 P.M. Bulova Watch Time!"

I left Drake University when my father died and I got a job as an announcer in Des Moines. That was not only the first announcement I made over the radio but for months after it was the only announcement the station manager would allow me to make. I'm glad I made the announcement only at 9:00. Had I been assigned to do the 7:30 or 8:30 time announcement I'm not sure I could have done it. Back then, I was not great at ad libbing. I'm still not but now I have Bruce, Colleen, Bonnie, and Marian to hide behind.

But about my childhood. I have been hooked on broadcasting since Uncle Chris made a crystal set by winding wire around an oatmeal box. I used to walk around Albia, muttering to myself, pretending that I was Milton Cross announcing the music for—excuse the expression, Kroger!—the A & P Gypsies.

That is the way growing up was back in Monroe County, Iowa. I won't claim to be a farm boy, but I'm not a city slicker, either. I lived in Albia. My father was a druggist there. Together with my two sisters and two brothers I grew up in that little village located seventy miles southeast of Des Moines. You can't call it the biggest city in the state. When the mapmakers print Albia, they use the smallest type they can find.

Albia was—and is—an alert little community. A few years back when I appeared in a newsreel with Ginger Rogers, Albia went all out. Royce Winkelman, the manager of the King Theatre in my hometown, got a print of the picture from somewhere, invited all my relatives in, and had a special showing. That wasn't the first time I had appeared as an entertainer in Albia. The way my mother told it, just about the time buttons replaced Pampers in my wardrobe, I rode my tricycle down the main street, and, as my mother sighed, "He was naked as a jaybird." She did say that my act was well received.

Or, as they say in commercials these days: "What's a mother to do!"

When I wasn't hanging around the courthouse square where the bandstand was or out on Uncle Chris's farm, I would either be listening to the radio or walking around, muttering to myself, pretending —as I said—to be a radio announcer.

Also, when the moon was full, I got interested in girls, but that's later. That was when I met Marge and gave up Betty Fairfield who had never answered my letters anyway. How did I meet Marge? Well, we were both riding our ponies into the schoolyard, there she was ahead of me, her black hair flying in the breeze, I followed her, and I've been following her ever since. After I met Marge, Betty Fairfield didn't have a Chinaman's chance with me.

But this is about my childhood, so let's get the show on the road. Well, because I was hooked I listened to everything radio had to offer. I listened, for example, to "Amanda of Honeymoon Hill." The soap opera used to start with the announcer saying, "The story of love and marriage in America's romantic South . . . the story of Amanda and Edward Leighton!" When the soap opera first went on the air, the announcer used to say, "Amanda of Honeymoon

Hill, laid in a world few Americans know." They
changed that introduction *fast!*

Sometimes as I wandered around Albia, Iowa, kicking cans and collecting stares because I was muttering to myself, I would pretend I was Bill Hay who
introduced Amos 'n' Andy each evening by saying:
"Here they ah!"

I suppose there is something unsettling about passing a small boy who is kicking a can and muttering,
"Here they ah, here they ah, here they ah . . ." But
suppose Bill Hay had got run over by a steamroller
and they needed a replacement? I wanted to be
ready. A guy couldn't spend the rest of his life kicking cans through Albia, could he?

Also, I would sit around my father's drugstore and
upset the customers by saying things like: "Buzz me,
Miss Blue."

"Check and double-check."

"I'se regusted."

I thought the Kingfish was the greatest man ever to
come down the pike. Had his lodge, the Mystic
Knights of the Sea, operated a chapter in Iowa, I
would have joined instantly. After I had sat around
the drugstore muttering Amos 'n' Andy things for
a while, my father would send me out to kick the can
some more.

As you can see, there was always something to do
in Albia—unless you ran out of cans.

I don't think the people of Albia knew *why* I was
muttering. They didn't know I was hooked on radio.
They figured I was an apprentice village idiot. But
they didn't throw stones at me or make fun. Live

and let live. That's the motto of the good people of
Albia. For a while I stopped being Bill Hay and started
being Harlow Wilcox who announced the Ben Bernie
Show. Ben Bernie had real class, especially when he
signed off with: "This is Ben Bernie, ladies and gen-
tlemen, and all the lads, wishing you a bit of pleasant
dreams. May good luck and happiness, success, good
health attend your schemes. And don't forget! Should
you ever send in your requests, why . . . we'll be sure
to do our best. Yowsah. Au revoir, a fond cheerio, a
bit of tweet tweet, God bless you, and pleasant
dreams. . . ."

When a kid had Ben Bernie around, who needed
Noel Coward!

Once, to impress a date, I stood on her front porch
and told her goodnight the way Ben Bernie did. But
I don't think she felt the same as I did about Mr.
Bernie. By the time I had reached the part that goes
"success, good health attend your schemes," she was
in the house with the screen door hooked. If she had
stayed around for the fond cheerio and the tweet
tweet I could have won her over.

How hooked was—and am—I on broadcasting?
Well, do you realize that I am the only one in my
neighborhood today who remembers that Chester
Morris once played the role of Boston Blackie in the
radio serial? Remember how that program used to
come on with the announcer saying: "Boston Blackie!
Friend of those who need a friend! Enemy of those
who make him an enemy!"?

Powerful stuff. Could Shakespeare have done
better?

Some people now question that Chester Morris

ever did play that role of Boston Blackie on the radio in addition to his playing that role in the movies. But according to one cast list, I'm right: Morris originated the radio character when he played it one summer as a replacement program for Amos 'n' Andy.

I listened to—and believed in—Buck Rogers, too. Buck Rogers in the twenty-fifth century! Now, there was drama you could sink your teeth into. Who needed Hollywood stars when I had Wilma Deering? Of course, she was really the girl friend of Buck Rogers, but at the time I was trying to make Betty Fairfield jealous. And do you remember how awful Killer Kane was? And how nice—at times—Black Barney was? Doctor Huer had invented the atomic disintegrator pistol as well as the molecular expansor and contractor beams. I was the first kid in Albia to become a Buck Rogers solar scout and to receive a planetary map. I would have gone to the moon but my mother didn't allow me to cross streets.

I remember once going out the back door and before I could get away, my mother called: "Where are you off to now?"

"To Mars," I answered.

"All right," she said. "But stay on the block."

Space travel, then as now, wasn't easy, especially with mothers around.

Today when we see the name Agnes Moorehead, we sit up and take notice, because she is a humdinger of an actress. But *I* remember her playing a role in "Bulldog Drummond." That show sure had a scary opening. A foghorn, eerie footsteps, the chiming of Big Ben, and the announcer saying: "Out of the

fog . . . out of the night . . . into his American ad-
ventures . . . comes . . . Bulldog Drummond!"

Whew!

"Why do you listen to that stuff?" my father complained once.

"Because he is making the streets of Albia safe to
play on," I said.

My father just gave me a look—and went back to
the drugstore to mix ice cream sodas for the evening
rush hour which, in Albia, lasted all of three minutes.

On which program did Van Heflin make his radio
debut? It was the "Court of Human Relations." On
what program did Jack Benny make *his* radio debut?
You'll never guess in a million years! The Ed Sullivan
Radio Show—back in May of 1931. Even back then
Ed Sullivan was responsible for a lot of broadcasting
firsts; he had the first radio appearances of Irving
Berlin, Jack Pearl, George M. Cohan, Colleen Sharp,
and Flo Ziegfeld. And *who*—of all people—used to
announce "Famous Jury Trials" back in those days?
Peter Grant.

Our entire family used to listen to Fibber McGee
and Molly. Wasn't radio beautiful back then? Who
could forget Fibber McGee's closet? And, when its
contents spilled out, who could forget Fibber muttering: "Gotta straighten out that closet one of these
days"?

People complain because *I* do the same show every
day! Those wonderful people did the same show
every time—with just enough variation to keep us
on our toes.

Remember the way Fibber said to the telephone
operator: "Oh, is that you, Myrt?"

When I said that once to our operator in Albia, my mother heard me, and I wasn't allowed out for a week. I guess our operator's name wasn't Myrt.

Remember the classic lines of Molly—"T'ain't funny, McGee!"

"Heavenly days!"

"How do you do, I'm sure!"

I was lucky to grow up during that golden moment of radio listening. Radio was the only noise we had; there was no television. The noise of radio filled our days. The voice of Boake Carter boomed each evening out of the air, straight into our Iowa kitchen. H. V. Kaltenborn talked to us every day. And I wonder how many times my mother, sisters, brothers, and I sat around the kitchen table and were whisked via our imaginations to the "Little Theater Off Times Square." We were the First Nighters—from Albia. I wonder how many times we were shown to our seats in that imaginary theater. We always arrived just in the nick of time, too. And I wonder how many times at intermission did the usher shout at us: "Smoking in the downstairs and outer lobbies only, please!"

Our family attended many such dramas, simply by sitting around our kitchen table. As Lawrence Welk would say: "Wunnerful, wunnerful."

Our social life was planned around radio.

"Want to build a snowman after dinner?" a neighbor's kid would say.

"What—and miss Fred Allen?" I would say.

Because Fred Allen visited us once a week, regular as clockwork, bringing with him Portland Hoffa, Titus Moody, Mrs. Nussbaum, Falstaff Openshaw—and hordes of others. I heard Frank Sinatra for the first

time on the Fred Allen Show. That's where I met
Connie Haines, Beatrice Kay, Jerry Colonna, Izzy
Kadetz, and Garry Moore.

And once a week I would visit—via radio—Grand
Central Station, which I figured had to be bigger
than the depot Albia possessed. I can still hear the
announcer opening the program:

"As a bullet seeks its target, shining rails in every
part of our great country are aimed at Grand Central
Station; heart of the nation's greatest city! Drawn by
a magnetic force—the fantastic metropolis—day and
night great trains rush toward the Hudson River,
down its eastern banks for 140 miles, flash briefly
past the long red rows of tenements south of 125th
Street, dive with a roar into the two-and-a-half-mile
tunnel which burrows beneath the glitter and swank
of Park Avenue, and then . . . GRAND . . . CENTRAL
. . . STATION!!! CROSSROADS . . . OF . . . A . . .
MILLION . . . PRIVATE . . . LIVES!!!"

I always felt sad that the trains made an entrance
that was a little less grand than that when they
tooted into Albia. The trouble with Albia, I felt, was
that it lacked the Hudson River, the long red rows
of tenements south of 125th Street, the swank and
glitter of Park Avenue, and most of all, that two-and-
a-half-mile tunnel for the train to enter Albia on.

One of the other kids in town pointed out that if
the train did go into a tunnel that long out on the
outskirts of Albia, by the time it got out of the tunnel
it would have missed Albia completely.

"That would confuse people waiting for the Bur-
lington," the know-it-all pointed out.

That whole discussion ended on a sour note. We

stood on the sidewalk, screaming angry things at one another about the swank and glitter of Park Avenue.

When I was not thinking about the swank and glitter of you-know-where I would be caught up with the Green Hornet. As soon as I heard the "Flight of the Bumble Bee" I knew the Green Hornet had come to save the day. Incidentally, the first actor to play the role of the Green Hornet was Al Hodge, who played the role of Captain Video later in television. I can still hear the announcer announcing: "He hunts the biggest of all game! Public enemies who try to destroy America! The Green . . . Hornet . . . Strikes . . . Again!"

You must admit that was heady stuff. Us kids in Albia slept better knowing the Green Hornet was on our side. If he didn't get the enemies of America, Bulldog Drummond did. Life was easier those days, wasn't it?

For my money, though, Jack Armstrong—the All American Boy!—was the greatest. As I said, I used to write love letters to Betty Fairfield, but she never answered. I guess she and Jack had a real serious thing going. But, loyal and true, hiding my breaking heart, I went around raising the flag for Hudson High every chance I got. I sent in boxtops and got a Jack Armstrong whistling ring, a Jack Armstrong Hike-O-Meter, a Jack Armstrong Secret Decoder, and—hold on to your hats!—a Jack Armstrong Norden Bombsight!

When I got all *that* my mother looked at me thoughtfully and said: "Now don't do anything foolish." I promised not to.

My mother liked radio, too. In 1942 when Joyce

Jordan, Girl Intern, got promoted to Joyce Jordan,
M.D., my mother was beside herself. The thing I
remember now about that show is that the role of
Dr. Mildermaul—which sounds almost as bad as Dr.
Seymour Heine when you think about it—was played
by Ed Begley. My mother was an avid radio listener.
Whenever Kate Smith went over the mountain, my
mother went, too.

Actually, my mother, whose name was Katherine
and whom I affectionately called Kate, was one of my
first boosters in radio. I'm sure she knew I had no
talent, but she would always encourage me: "If that's
your dream, go fight for it."

Then there was Uncle Chris. Now, he believed in
his heart that Lum and Abner were for real. He
thought there actually was a store called the Jot 'em
Down Store. He thought there actually was a place
on the map called Pine Ridge, Arkansas. Well, we
tried to convince him the store and town were imaginary, but in 1936 when Waters, Arkansas, up and
changed its name to Pine Ridge, there was no holding
Uncle Chris. To him, if the town existed, the store
existed. And if the store existed, Lum and Abner
existed. And if Lum and Abner existed, so did Cedric
Weehunt. Uncle Chris was all for hopping a bus and
giving Cedric a piece of his mind!

And *I* remember when Orson Welles played the
Shadow! I depended on the Shadow to know what evil
lurked in the hearts of men because I figured that
the Green Hornet and Bulldog Drummond couldn't
be looking out for Albia round the clock. It gave me
a comfortable feeling to know that one of my best
(radio) friends was a mysterious stranger who had

learned how to cloud men's minds hypnotically so they couldn't see him. Albia had a few other cases where men got their minds clouded, but that didn't happen much after they came and arrested the bootlegger. The bootlegger actually made magic more powerful than the Shadow. The Shadow clouded minds so people couldn't see him. When the bootlegger clouded minds, the guys with the clouded minds couldn't see anything!

That's why I stick with Diet Pepsi, but this is about my radio childhood, isn't it?

Well, lady, other than people like the Shadow, the Green Hornet, and those others, you might say that I grew up in a Vic and Sade kind of world which no longer exists. I lived in the little house halfway up in the next block. Rush Gook—Vic and Sade's boy—had Uncle Fletcher; but *I* had Uncle Chris! Remember Uncle Fletcher? He used to hang out at the Bright Kentucky Hotel and watch the trains go by. Whenever he spoke of anyone, he usually added the comment: ". . . Later died!"

The people in the world of Vic and Sade had their counterparts in Albia and small towns everywhere. There was Dottie Brainfeeble, Chuck Brainfeeble, and the Brick-Mush Man. There was Chester Gumpos, the garbage man. There was Smelly Clark, Bluetooth Johnson, and Mr. Buller. Can you ever forget Sade's friend Ruthie Stembottom, who went to all the washrag sales at Yamelton's Department Store? And Ishingan Fishigan of Sishigan, Michigan? Or Robert and Slobert Heeg—identical twins?

Yes, the radio of my childhood was real—and broadcasting hooked me. Radio brought the world to

our small town and on Sunday, October 30, 1938, it
sent our world running for the storm cellars. We
were listening to Orson Welles and the Mercury
Theater. The program that night was Howard Kock's
adaptation of H. G. Wells's *War of the Worlds.* We
thought Iowa—as well as the swank and glitter of
Park Avenue—was being invaded by creatures from
outer space.

When did I decide to stop kicking tin cans, muttering to myself, and writing letters to Betty Fairfield—
giving all that up to go into radio for real? I suppose
I actually decided there might be a niche—however
small—for me in broadcasting the first time I heard
Martin Block's "Makebelieve Ballroom." Record-spin-
ning had come of age! This was the first record show
on the radio networks. And it just occurred to me: I
had one of the first record shows on the television
networks!

Radio, radio, radio!

And *now,* television!

Wunnerful, wunnerful!

Broadcasting holds a magic for me. I'll always be
hooked. All my life I have been coming here to WLW-
Television and the morning show. Well, the Lord has
been good to me.

He got me here.

Next question, please.

# 4.

# *Paul Baby &*

# EARLY
# TELEVISION

☆ "I've been hooked on you," a lady from Middletown said the other day, "since you first came on television. I'll bet you are glad things have settled down since those early days, aren't you?"

Television *settled down?*

Mercy!

Still, she has a point. A lot of television has changed. Most of the stuff we see on the tube is on film or video tape. Few programs are "live" these days. WLW-Television cranks out more "live" programs than most stations. Thus, the era when Betty Furness could make a coast-to-coast booboo is over. Thanks to film and tape, which can be corrected, errors are edited out and you never see them.

57

Except—that is—on the Dixon Show. Lady, we're televised "live." That's us you see on the tube, us as we are actually happening.

The mistakes we make, you see. Period. There is no way on earth for us to *un*televise a goof. When I hold up one product for the camera and talk about another one, that's it, lady. We can't go back and start over. I just sit there, looking dumb as usual, with egg on my face. We can't edit what you see in your living room. You can pull the shades and hide. Not us. We are the way all television used to be: live.

And there we are each morning at nine, with our bare faces hanging out.

A network executive visiting our show said to me: "Paul, your show is a ninety-minute accident that's just waiting to happen."

He's right, but would a Dixon Show without an accident be the Dixon Show that hooks you? I don't think so. When we hit the air each morning I am sure of only two things: Kneesville—and an audience made up of the most beautiful women in the world. Ever since I first stepped in front of that first television camera, I have been surrounded—and blessed—by accidents.

A few of them, like being in the same studio with an elephant that hadn't been toilet trained and that was much too big for Pampers, still make me shudder and reach for the Anacin bottle. This took place years ago when I started in television. A live elephant advertising the Shrine Circus had been brought into the studio. So far, so good. But there's something about me that brings out the beast in animals and the worst in elephants. There I was, being hoisted

by the elephant's trunk, and there was the elephant
using the studio floor for a john.

The station janitor took one look and left in anger.

"I ain't cleaning up after no doggone elephant!"
he shouted, announcing his retirement from show
business. I don't think he said *doggone*. Rather, he
said something in Italian that I don't think I'll put
into this book.

But did things like that happen only during the
"good old days" of television? Lady, things like that
still happen on the Dixon Show but thank goodness
they no longer happen with elephants. I'm not suggesting that the 150 in our audience each morning
are not housebroken. I suggest only that each morning I expect—and get—the unexpected.

Consider the morning I was doing my commercial
for White Cloud bathroom tissue. Some lady in the
bleachers stood up, waved, and shouted for my attention. What other show lets the women interrupt
the commercials? Anyway, I let her have the floor—
and what happened?

She yacked on and on about her collection of—of
all things—bathroom tissue from Europe.

"I even have a sample of the bathroom tissue from
Liechtenstein," she shouted.

"Swell, lady," I muttered.

"Some of the tissue from Germany feels like sand-
paper," she shouted. "Here. *Feel* it."

"I'll take your word for it, lady," I said.

"The tissue from Buckingham Palace is the rough-
est, though," she shouted. "No wonder everyone goes
around over there saying 'God save the Queen!' "

So there you are. Maybe television *has* changed

since the "good old days," but not on our show. The only difference is that back then none of us knew what we were doing and back then we admitted it; today we still don't know what we're doing, but we like to pretend that we do. Pretend hard enough and you get appointed program director!

When the Paul Dixon Show first went on the network, wrestling and women on roller skates were all the rage. Hopalong Cassidy was king and so was Super Circus—with Mary Hartline. Remember her long, blonde hair? She was the Veronica Lake of the test patterns. Cisco Kid was on every other channel. And for intellectuals, there was a program called "You Asked For It." And, suddenly from nowheresville, there I was, on the tube.

The critics were kinder to me than I deserved. Do I keep a scrapbook? You betcha!

Val Adams wrote in *The New York Times* that "Paul Dixon is a refreshing addition to eastern viewing." Edmund Leamy said in the New York *Telegram* that our show "bubbled over with so much enthusiasm, freshness, and charm that it lifts you out of yourself." And Sid Chalit in the New York *Daily News* announced that "one of the most refreshing platter-pushers is a gent out of Cincinnati tagged Paul Dixon. He has poise, deftness, and a good professional touch."

"Is that really me?" I asked Marge, bewildered.

"They must have been watching women wrestlers," Marge said. "They have more poise than you do. And talent."

"I suppose," I said, relieved. That sure didn't *sound* like me but it was nice of New York writers to say so.

You see, I don't believe in press notices, however flattering they are. Many television personalities *did* believe their press notices—and where are they now? Gone! I guess they took their poise and left. Me, I took my poise with a grain of salt.

Anyway, in the early days the true critics of the Paul Dixon Show were not on newspaper payrolls. I might have fooled a few newspaper guys, but I couldn't fool my viewers—especially one farmer-turned-critic. He saw our show, got out his tractor, hitched the plow, and chugged across his back forty, plowing. He plowed so thoroughly he plowed up the coaxial cable that carried our show from Cincinnati to the network.

He said he didn't cut our cable intentionally, but he seemed more cheerful than sad. Well, that's show business. If the New York critics don't get you, a farmer with a plow will!

Back then, television was casual. Although our show started each afternoon at two, from noon until seconds before two you would have found the entire Dixon crew—Wanda Lewis, Dottie Mack, and later Sis Camp, plus me—in a little Italian restaurant a stone's throw from the WCPO-TV studios. Also our producer would be there. And cameramen. And prop men. Were we discussing the show? Guess again, lady. We were playing shuffleboard! We'd arrive at the studios as our theme was playing. That is how casual television was back then!

But never let it be said that when I first stepped in front of a television camera I was a newcomer to that sort of thing. Few of you know that I am an actor who has trod the boards—if that is what actors are supposed to do with the boards, whatever the boards are, I mean. Yes, lady, I was actually on the stage. Actually in a play. In case you missed me, I played the role of C. K. Dexter Haven in *Philadelphia Story*. I didn't play the role on Broadway. Would you believe Fort Thomas, Kentucky? Would you believe the Highland High School auditorium? I played the role three nights in May, 1948. Since no one has asked me to do another play, I have yet to return to the stage.

But I am still available. Does that help?

*And,* shortly after *that,* I went to Hollywood and made my first movie. Although I have not made a Hollywood movie since, I still do not consider that my last movie. I like to consider it my first movie. Has a nicer ring to it, wouldn't you say?

In case you missed me on the stage in Fort Thomas, Kentucky—and frankly, a large number of people *did*—perhaps you saw me star in the Hollywood movie. The movie, which was released in 1951, was *Disc Jockey,* which I was back then. Ginny Simms starred in the picture with me. So did Tom Drake, Jane Nigh, Michael O'Shea, Russ Morgan, Tommy Dorsey, Sarah Vaughan, and Herb Jeffries. Come to think of it, they all starred *more* than I did. I was lost in a crowd of twenty-eight other disc jockeys starring in the movie, too. To be honest, if you sneezed once during the movie, you missed me completely. But if you sneezed, I do hope you used Scotties. A lot of people must have sneezed during the showing of my Hollywood movie because so few of you remember my movie career.

I'm also in a bunch of home movies, too, if that

helps. I show them every time we have company, which makes the company leave early. I think it's because Marge isn't a good hostess. She sits and laughs at the movies—in the serious places, too.

The guests don't laugh. They don't say anything. They sit in silence and sometimes when the lights are off and the movie is unwinding on the screen, they get their coats and sneak home.

To show you what a box office attraction I was in Cincinnati when *Disc Jockey* opened, it opened as one half of a double feature. Also playing was *Sierra Passage* with Wayne Morris and Lola Albright. *Their* picture was advertised as "Wild gold country's strangest manhunt"; *my* picture was advertised as a "Riotous romance of showland." The movie wasn't that riotous and as for it being a romance, they wouldn't let me kiss the girl stars. The movie was such a dog that it has yet to play on television.

I know—because I keep watching for it.

But back to "early television." Just how my radio program moved bodily from radio into television is explained in Dick Perry's book *Vas You Ever in Zinzinnati?* Perry knows whereof he speaks because he had the misfortune to wander into the television studio when the Dixon Show was first being fed to the network. To show how casual life was, before he left two hours later he had been hired to write my show!

What I mean is, back then things were hectic. The program director doubled as a clown on a kiddie show. And you'll never guess who was making our stage sets. That's right! Uncle Al! Or rather, Al Lewis. He had yet to become Uncle Al. Anyway, Perry's account of those days appears in his book about Cincinnati. He wrote:

> I stood in the control room, watched Dixon "perform," turned to Mort [Watters] and said:
> "Write what?"
> Paul, ad libbing a commercial for Fritos, shocked my commercial nature by saying they tasted stale. Wanda Lewis was holding a cue card that Paul was ignoring, Dottie Mack was giggling about something, and the two floor men—one was Jack Tempfer who before television had been a streetcar motorman— were playing cards, oblivious to the action. Only Cowan and Sternberg, the cameramen, paid attention but they had to. Well, the engineers in the control room were paying attention a little, but they seemed more concerned about something called "night maintenance" than the show.
> "This isn't Chicago television," Watters told me. "This is Cincinnati television. . . ."

Though Dixon was an exuberant critter not given to reading scripts, still my job of "writing" those Dixon shows was a snap. Paul's talent was and is ad libbing and letting the laughs, if any, fall where they may. But he needed a studio audience (I'm glad Avco gave him one) and when I came to WCPO-TV he had no audience. I wasn't worried, though. The pay was good and, anyway, I needed a job at the time.

The Dumont Network had just signed the Dixon Show on the network opposite Arthur Godfrey and Ernie Kovacs, which meant only the master control room in New York was watching us. But Dixon wasn't worried about that. He worried about "getting rolling."

"Cincinnatians know the kind of show we do," he fretted. "But in other cities . . ."

I decided the best thing to write for him was to write absolutely nothing. Had I written anything, he would have made hash of it, and besides, that wasn't his kind of show. So each Wednesday night before the program Dixon and I would meet and I'd give him three five-by-seven index cards, a one-line joke on each.

"Keep them handy," I said. "If you find yourself running out of steam, use one."

The plan worked like a charm. Each week Dixon and I met and I gave him three jokes. Since he hadn't used the jokes from the week before, I kept giving him the same three jokes I started with. After all, as long as he had something to fall back on, he didn't worry, and he could relax and do the show as he'd always done.

After a year of writing the Dixon Show that way, I quit and took the three jokes with me, my reputation as a comedy writer intact.

Before Perry left to become a novelist and historian (he wrote the only history of Cincinnati that contains one-liners!) he served for a while as our producer. He was as casual in his production methods as he was as comedy writer and historian. One night, thirty minutes before we were to go on the network, Perry showed up with the entire Naval ROTC Glee Club from Ohio's Miami University.

"The idea of a glee club sounded nice for the show," he explained. "We'll fit them in somewhere. Don't know where we'll put that many people, though."

Our studio had no room for a glee club. And we couldn't put them outside in the parking lot and take pictures of them from there; it was raining cats and dogs. But talk about a flurry of activity! The remote crew was alerted, the remote truck—and the glee club—took off like birds to the Cincinnati Gas & Electric Company Auditorium because someone remembered we happened to have a line from there to the station. Just in the nick of time, when Perry cued them on the air, the picture of them blinked in from the remote setup.

"You see," said Perry. "Things work out, don't they? What was everyone fussing about?"

Years later Perry and I were sitting around, drinking Diet Pepsi, and reminiscing. Our conversation turned to the studio audience we have now. Perry shook his head in wonderment.

"We were supposed to be so brilliant," he said, "but, Paul, do you realize not one of us thought about getting a studio audience for you?"

We looked at one another, surprised.

The thought had not occurred to me, either.

"Well," I said, "give John Murphy credit for that. It was his idea to have a studio audience. That just shows you, Dick. I owe a lot to a lot of people, but it took John Murphy to come along at just the right time and find the right niche for me."

I mean that, too. If it hadn't been for guys like Mort Watters and then John Murphy, I don't know where I'd be today. I certainly wouldn't be here. Television, the people in it, and you viewers have all done much better by me than I'll ever be able to do by you. Can you see now why I can't get a big head? I'm where I am today only because so many other people helped me. I didn't get here by myself. So thank God for you girls out there with your shades pulled and your television sets on, and thank God for the people behind the cameras. Without the both of you, I'd be nothing.

Those early days had serious moments, too. Some

of you girls who watch today appeared on those early Dixon shows when you were kids. And you'll know exactly who you are, too! I'm talking about those of you who in the 1950's held backyard carnivals for the polio fund. Each afternoon a group of children would appear to give the money you had earned. One year you raised by yourselves $10,000 for our show alone!

But who was it who tried to get me elected the treasurer of Hamilton County in 1953? I'll admit that I did not win by a landslide. In fact, I didn't win at all. I was a write-in candidate. I *did* get *one* vote. That's all another write-in candidate got, too, so I didn't feel bad. His name was Douglas MacArthur.

"When Paul Dixon and the television camera first got together," Mary Wood wrote in the *Cincinnati Post,* "it was a monumental case of instant rapport which has been going ever since. Paul and television were made for each other. He's a beguiling clown with unquenchable good humor who has a rare ability to light up a television screen and make his audience know they're going to have a good time."

But the Dumont Network is no more—and maybe I helped bury it. I might have helped kill off live television on the ABC television network, too. But those, my friends, were the "good old days." Al Hodges was Captain Video. Dumont carried the New York fights on Monday night. Bishop Sheen came on to take some of Milton Berle's audience. Paul Whiteman conducted his TV Teen Club. Sundays were reserved for Edward R. Murrow's "See It Now."

Also, in Cincinnati a young man was working around our studios. Fresh from the army—and a

Ludlow, Kentucky, native, and (then) quite single—
he was and still is a handsome devil. Used to be a
lifeguard at Coney Island. His initials are Bob Braun.
We'll have more about him later. Can you wait? Try
hard.

Just as Bob Braun was part of our early television
scene, so was Dean Miller, who later starred in "De-
cember Bride." Do you remember? We worked together at WCPO-TV. And so did Glenn Ryle before
he became Skipper Ryle. Add the dapper and most
happy fellow by the name of Len Goorian—and what
you will have will be the good old days of television—
but the good old days are still going full blast at
WLW-Television because "live" is the word for Avco.

A lady asked me if I have been in television so long
that the excitement of doing a live show is gone.
Well, I told her the same thing I'll tell you.

When I no longer feel excitement doing the Dixon
Show, I'll be dead. I mean that. I still get nervous
before each show. And after each show, I'm ex-
hausted. I'm drained—physically and emotionally.
My shirt is soaking wet. Those cameras take a lot out
of a person.

So I guess I can never become hard-shelled about
this business. After each show, I still telephone Marge
—for her reaction. Yes, lady, she *does* watch. That
girl hasn't missed me on the air except when she took
time off to have Pam and Greg.

All I know is, when television began, a slick performer with a golden voice and a theatrical manner
came up to me, smoothed his hair, cleared his throat,
and intoned: "Relax, Dixon. Wait a month. You'll get
over that Midwest nervousness of yours."

I told Marge that. All she did was look at me—with love—and shake her head.

"What does that mean?" I said.

"It means," she said, "that if you ever start acting like Mr. Show Business, buster, I'll belt you."

Me get over my nervousness in a month or so? Mister, you told me that years ago—and it never happened.

Next question, please.

# 5.

## *Paul Baby's*

# AUDIENCE AND STUDIO

☆ "What happens when we arrive at your dumb show?"

The question is reasonable. Since we started at WLW-Television more than 546,000 women have been in our studio audience. But some who can't make the trip and those still waiting are bound to be curious about what will happen when they *do* arrive at the station before the show.

Well, between 7:30 and 8:30 each weekday morning, our lobby at WLW-Television resembles a rush hour at Grand Central Station—but with this difference: the rush hour is composed of the most beautiful women in the world.

70

Of course, not *all* of you are beautiful women; some of you are husbands looking bewildered and wondering what to make of the cackling. You should hear the cackling in our lobby. You women make more noise with your cackles than the chickens did the morning someone said Uncle Chris poured bourbon in the laying mash.

And since some of you travel a far piece to get here, several of you will arrive the night before. However, most of you leave your homes early that morning, sometimes as early as two. As early as seven, you straggle into our lobby sleepy-eyed. There you sit, pooped, yawning, and wondering if our show is worth the effort.

Some of you not familiar with the Cincinnati expressway system end up in Kentucky before you realize that you've goofed. A few have got as far as Louisville. There you sit, just like the early arrivals at the studio, pooped, yawning, and wondering if our show is worth the effort.

Actually, all day long the lobby at our station is one grand traffic jam—and here's why.

First, you girls wait there to see our show. Although our show is off the air at 10:30 you won't return to the lobby until around 10:45 because after the show we pass out the loot in the studio. Since you didn't arrive loaded, you've made up your minds to go home that way! By the time you return to the lobby—and while you're still in the studio, in fact—a studio crew is ripping our set to shreds and putting up the set for the 50-50 Club. We both use the same studio. And once you have returned downstairs to the lobby, you run smack dab into more of the 50-50 Club doings:

the early arrivals for Bob's show are sitting where you sat—and making just as much noise.

Later, when the 50-50 Club ladies are released from the studio, they come back down to the lobby and run into the early arrivals for Vivienne Della Chiesa's Afternoon Show. In other words, lady, during the day our lobby ain't the best place to catch forty winks!

Consider also that when the Dixon Show audience, the 50-50 Club audience, and the Afternoon Show audience are crowding our lobby, other groups are waiting there for other shows! Audiences for shows like "It's Academic" wait for their shows to be taped. But, lady, if you think our lobby is crowded, you should see the mission across the street. While some of you are waiting to come upstairs, you get impatient. That's when you cross the street, enter the mission, and are never heard from again!

Where was I? Oh yes, what happens before the show?

Well, somehow or other by 8:30 our lobby is filled with women gabbing and husbands muttering. At that moment you meet our beautiful hostess, Dottie Hope, who makes you welcome and sees that you are comfortable. Dottie explains to the husbands that things are not as bad as they seem. Then you are escorted to the elevator which will whisk you upstairs to the studio. A word of caution: this is an elevator and *not* the studio. One lady walked into the elevator, looked around, and complained: "I thought Paul Baby did his show from a bigger place!" Once in the studio you might see Bruce Brownfield rehearsing with his musicians. Or, you might see Scratchy (when he is not giving out autographs) setting up the com-

mercial props. You might see cameramen checking
out cameras; Gordy going over last-minute changes;
Alice straightening my desk; Colleen, Bonnie, or
Marian rehearsing a song; or—if you've lingered too
long at the mission—you stagger into the studio, see
nothing, and fall sound asleep.

Well, once you are *in* the studio, you climb high
into the bleacher seats and—if you're a girl—you
adjust your skirt for Kneesville. If you're a man, you
watch the girls adjust their skirts. After you've settled in your seat, you wonder how on earth the program will ever get on the air because all around you
is utter confusion. You are not alone in this wondering. Each morning I wonder the same thing. But the
one who wonders—and worries—the most is John
Murphy.

As you sit in the bleachers before the show starts,
listen to the chatter around you. You'll get a kick out
of comments.

"The studio looks different, doesn't it?"

Or:

"Isn't Scratchy cute!"

Or:

"I think we left the headlights on!"

Depending upon how you imagined our studio to
be, chances are it will seem too big or too small. And
even if you watch us in color, you will be amazed by
the additional color splashed around the place. But
you will also see how terribly make-believe the Dixon
Show set is. Behind the great "flats," the walls of our
set, you will see stage braces: two-by-four pieces of
wood that (hopefully) hold our world together. Over-
head you will see a tangle of lights like a Hollywood

movie set. And wherever you look, you will see people running around like chickens with their heads cut off. They look as if they don't know what they're doing or why they're there.

This figures! On our show no one does know exactly what he's doing. That's what makes the Dixon Show fun.

As the show unfolds, many of your questions will be answered. Why is that? Well, to be honest, there are some things that happen on the show off camera that the viewer at home never gets to see. Many things happen in our studio that bewilder the viewer at home.

Example: when some of you wave at the camera, you don't wave at the camera, but out into space. And the viewers at home wonder why. I'm glad the viewers at home wondered that. It gives me a chance to answer one of the few technical questions I can answer.

No, lady. The ones who wave off in the distance haven't been to the mission. You see, our studio has several television sets that face the studio audience so they can see what the viewer at home sees. These sets are called monitors. When the camera takes a picture of the studio audience, the girls look at themselves in these monitors to see how pretty they are. That is why, when the camera focuses on them, their eyes are focused on the monitor—and so that's where they wave—at themselves in living color.

On the other hand, when we take a look at Kneesville at the start of each program, we don't have that problem because when we take pictures of your knees, your knees don't care which is the camera and which is the monitor. I think that's because knees don't wave. If you look in some morning and *do* see wavy knees, adjust your set.

The trouble is *not* with the knees!

Could it be that you stayed too long at the mission?

One other technical thing: you hear me refer to the "hod." To be frank, this is not *that* technical, because if it were I would be unable to explain it. The hod is the stand on which we place commercial props so the camera can take a picture of them. And if Scratchy is on the ball—which he usually is—the right commercial prop appears with the right commercial. Oh, sometimes it might appear upside down or sideways, but on our show it's the thought that counts. We ain't no big fat Hollywood production.

Speaking of Hollywood productions, though, we once had a program director who tried to turn our show into one. He didn't get too far. I'll never forget the afternoon he strutted into my office and announced that it didn't look "professional" for me to stay behind the desk with my bare face hanging out while I delivered commercial announcements.

"That's not the way we do things, sweetheart," he said.

"Oh," I said.

"You need a special commercial set," he crooned. "Here's the bit—" which I suppose is Hollywood talk "—from now on. When you do a commercial walk over to this lavish commercial set where everything will be laid out for you. Don't fret, sweetheart. I've ordered the carpenters to build you a commercial set that will be dreamy."

"That's not the way I am," I said. "And that's not the kind of show I do."

I was about to say more, like stop calling me *sweet-*

*heart,* because to be called *Paul Baby* is one thing, but to be called sweetheart by a guy wearing lavender slacks and a pink jacket is another. But he didn't give me a chance to go on.

"Sweetheart," he gasped, "don't you realize that when you do commercials from the desk where you do the rest of your show you look dumb?"

"Now you're getting the idea!" I said. "That's why we call it a dumb show. And do you mind *not* calling me sweetheart? It doesn't sound right and—"

But off he trotted to wherever program directors who wear lavender slacks trot to. And the next day, there in our studio—off to one side—was a lavish set before which he expected me to deliver commercials the way network announcers do.

And if you know me, there's one thing I ain't— and that's a network announcer, no matter whose sweetheart I am, kiddo!

Did I use his "dreamy" set?

Nope!

I went and did the same dumb show I always do, doing the commercials from the desk, same as ever, and using our $2.89 hod to hold commercial displays. The program director—that day wearing a heliotrope jacket, polka dot slacks, and a tie that looked like an orange pompom that had been left out in the rain— didn't say a word and neither did I. But the next day the commercial set was missing.

And three weeks later, the program director wasn't there, either. The station, reluctantly, had to let him go. The NBC peacock was getting jealous. Isn't that NBC peacock a sweetheart—if you'll pardon the expression?

Still, I don't want you to think that we don't maintain high production standards on the Dixon Show. Gordy wears a clean shirt every day, Scratchy combs his hair every chance he gets, and as for the hod— well, once a year we give it a coat of paint, whether it needs it or not.

So much for the technical secrets of our thing.

But look around the studio. A lot has happened in that old studio at WLW-Television. As I write this book the station is in the midst of a rebuilding program. By the time you read this, who knows? Perhaps we'll be doing our show from a newer studio that— according to the plans—will be a humdinger.

But I don't know. Call me sentimental if you want, but I like this old studio we have now.

If only its walls could talk, what stories they would tell!

Famous movie stars have walked through the same doors that you women come through each morning. All of the great political figures of our time—well, let's be honest, *most* all—have come through those same doors, too. For this, lady, is the same studio that Ruth Lyons used and this is where she enjoyed her finest hours. This is the studio where, Monday through Friday, she entertained thousands and thousands and thousands of her friends. People from all walks of life have walked through those doors and said hello to Mother.

And this is the studio that Candy knew.

And this is the studio from which Mother said good-by.

Oh, if only these old studio walls could talk!

Sometimes during quiet moments (though they are few and far between) I come here alone when the studio is empty and silent. No one will be in the

control room. No one will be in the bleacher seats. No
one will be in the staging area. The dozens of over-
heads will be turned off and cold; only a lone work-
light will cast long and lonely shadows. Silence will
be everywhere. It will be so quiet in here you can hear
a pin drop. That is the way this wonderful old studio
is.

When I come here during moments like that, I
climb as high as any of you in the studio audience, up
there to the last row in the bleachers. There I sit and
stare down at the emptiness and the dark of the staging area. There is no sound, but sometimes in my
heart I hear a hundred sounds—the remembered
sounds of old studio's yesterdays. In my heart I hear
Mother doing her show. I can hear the applause as she
steps out to greet her audience and as she sings:
"Let me entertain you . . ."

I can see her, in my mind's eye, rocking back and
forth in her chair and holding in her hands that microphone which is, of course, a garland of flowers.
And from my bleacher seat, I can smell the faint scent
of her perfume. And all around me, in the bleachers,
are the ghost murmurs of some long-ago audience,
ladies wearing white gloves, listening.

But most of all, I hear the voice of Mother: now
happy, now sad, now quarreling, now loving the
world, and now changing it. . . .

No, my friend. You are not the only one who misses
Mother. Every time I walk into this old and wonderful studio, I miss her, too. It is *her* studio, really. And
no matter how they doll it up or refurbish it, this
studio will always be hers.

Now can you see why—quite honestly—I can't

consider myself a great star, a fabulous talent, or a powerful force on television? How could I possibly be any of those things when each day I use the studio that held the greatest influence Midwest television will ever have!

# 6.

## *Paul Baby &*

## COMMERCIALS

☆ "Why don't other announcers do commercials the way you do?"

That's what the women ask me every time I turn around.

If you wonder the same thing, I've got news for you. Even *I* can't do commercials the way I do them. What I mean is, when I do a commercial, I never know exactly how it's going to turn out.

"You're not alone, wondering how they will turn out," Gordy our producer told me. "Advertising agencies don't know how your commercials are going to turn out, either. Neither do sponsors. And neither do we in the control room," he added. He seemed sad about something.

But do the advertising agency men worry?

And do the sponsors fret?

Nope.

Gordy and his crew, of course, worry—and with good reason. When they point a camera *here,* I might start talking about a product over *there.* This will upset an ordinary television crew, but WLW-Television has surrounded me with long-suffering geniuses. Whatever mess I get into, Gordy and his crew manage to rescue me and make me look better than I really am.

But as for my doing straight—and *ordinary*—commercials? Lady, I don't think I could do one if my life depended upon it. I'm not sure, though. The truth is, I haven't tried.

A program director, no longer in television, once complained to me: "Shape up, Paul. You make more mistakes than a kid fresh out of announcing school."

But Bill McCluskey, our client-service director who handles the sponsors for the Dixon Show, happened to wander by just then. He stopped and said: "Paul may make mistakes, but we'll just have to let him be himself. He can sell more products than ten network announcers you could name."

I'm not that good, but that's McCluskey for you: a kind word for everybody.

The program director, though, wasn't convinced. "But," he protested, "Dixon doesn't even follow the copy half the time."

I'm glad he didn't elaborate. The half the time I *do* follow the copy, I make a mess of it.

"Doesn't matter," said Bill. "Ask your agency contacts which is more important: following the copy or selling the product?"

The two of them didn't let me get a word in edge-

wise which was just as well. I would probably have
said the wrong thing *there*, too!

The point is that I'm not a golden-throated network
announcer—and I never will be. I can't—and wouldn't
—use fancy-Dan phrases to gab with you girls. All
I can do is be myself, not be a phony, and be honest
with you right down the line. I can't talk about products the way the network boys do. I wouldn't feel
right talking that way. I talk about products the same
way the guy down the street talks about something
that *he* believes in. I ain't no famous movie star who
can step up to the camera, adopt a grand pose, and
say "Hi there," going into a pitch. You'd laugh me out
of existence!

And listen, doing some of those commercials can
take a lot out of a guy. I'll never forget the time we
advertised that prune juice. Each time the announcement ran, I had to drink a glass of the stuff on
camera. You all know what happened. At the end of
the 13-week campaign when the sponsor wanted to
renew, I was too weak to tell him no. I was too weak
to say *anything!*

If you think poor Gordy has trouble keeping his
wits about him when he's producing the show, think
of what poor Bill McCluskey goes through. Though he
is one of the nicest and most respected fellows in the
industry, Bill has the most thankless job the industry
has to offer. As client-service director responsible for
the advertising you see on our show, he must visit
clients and advertising agencies in New York, Chicago, and other points, trying to explain the Dixon
Show to prospects who can only shake their heads
and look bewildered.

"Okay, Bill," they will say, "we're convinced Dixon

and the housewives are buddy-buddy. That's why we want to buy the show. But we want to run our filmed commercials."

Filmed commercials? Only on rare occasions with us. Toni uses them because I ain't good at putting my hair up at night. Pepsi-Cola uses them—now and then—because of the pretty girls in the girl-watching commercials. If we didn't run those girl-watching films, you men would sulk and I would too. Those girls ain't dogs.

When agencies suggest filmed commercials on our show, Bill McCluskey—except in the cases noted—does his best to convince them otherwise.

"Let Paul himself do your commercial live," he will suggest.

"But our filmed commercials cost $50,000 to make," they might murmur. "And you'd be amazed at the research and work that went into every frame of them. Can Dixon, just talking, do better than a film that cost a bundle?"

"Paul Dixon," Bill will continue, never giving up, "could sell your product just by standing in front of the camera and making a fool of himself."

"We'd have to see that to believe it," the agency men will say—and out to Cincinnati they come.

They see.

And they go back, shaking their heads, but *believing*.

You can't blame them for being skeptical. Those who see our show can't figure out what we do or why we stay on the air. We don't really do anything, do we? I sometimes wonder why we're successful, too. I don't question it, though. I just thank the good Lord that we are.

So pity the poor agency men when they come here to see our show. Then *they* have to go back and try to explain it to others. And they can't, either. Can you, lady? If you can, will you help us out: explain the show in twenty-five words or less and we'll be grateful. Bill McCluskey needs all the help he can get!

He even needs help when the agency men or clients visit Cincinnati. He knows and I know that when we're walking along the streets here, sure as shooting a full-grown man is going to shout from a passing car: "Hiya, Paul Baby!"

The first time that happened—and it happens lots —the New York agency man who was with us looked surprised. I had the feeling he was looking to see if I carried a purse.

"They always call me that," I explained, trying to console him.

"Ah," the agency man said.

"It means they're Paul's viewers," Bill added.

"Ah," the agency man said.

"Happens every time I walk down the street," I said.

"On the way back from lunch," the agency man said, "do you mind if we take a cab?"

We did—but the moment we climbed into the cab, the cab driver turned around, smiled a smile that went from ear to ear, and said: "Hiya, Paul Baby!"

Happily for me most advertisers and advertising agencies are used to me now. As one account executive, now a very good friend of mine, offered: "Paul, if we had a guy like you in every market, we wouldn't need filmed commercials at all."

I tend to question that because, as I said, even on our show we run filmed commercials now and then. Still, kind words like that are nice to hear.

Sponsors and agency men are reasonable guys and as human as the rest of us. Forget the highfalutin stuff you read about them in books and how Hollywood portrays them. They're serious businessmen and I have news for you: I have met advertisers and agency people from every part of the country and I assure you that the phonies are few and far between. They're like us. Good guys, trying to live decent lives so we can look at ourselves in the mirror each morning. They go home at night the same as your husbands do; and they worry about car payments, how Junior did in school, and—if they're from this area— I hope they relax with either a Diet Pepsi or a Burger Beer.

Also, agency men kid a lot. There was that time I was in New York talking with an advertising copywriter.

"Paul," he said, "I wish you wouldn't *invent* words."

"Me invent words?" I said. "Are you kidding? I don't know how to use half the words they got in the English language now."

"Guess again," he said. "Come over here."

He turned on a tape recorder on the far side of his office. Out came the sound part of a Pepsodent commercial I had done on the air.

"Ladies," I was saying, "here's the stuff that puts puzazz in your . . . ah . . . puzazz."

The copywriter stopped the tape a moment and said: "Paul, I don't think that's the way their campaign reads."

He started the tape again.

"And," I went on, "that's the trouble with most of you women. You ain't got no puzazz left."

The copywriter stopped the tape with a wince and

said: "That's not quite the way the copy goes, is it, Paul?"

We listened some more.

"Well, Pepsodent contains . . . ah . . . ah . . . Pepsodent contains qwertyuioplkjhgfdsa. And because of that, you get puzazz in your puzazz. No. I mean, you get puzazz in your teeth. What I'm trying to say is, you get puzazz in your smile. I guess that's what I'm trying to say. All I know, girls, is that Pepsodent is great. It contains qwertyuioplkjhgfdsa! So try it. I know you'll like it."

The copywriter turned the tape recorder off. "Do you realize, Paul," he said, "that if I *wrote* a commercial that way I would be drummed out of advertising? Pepsodent puts puzazz in your smile, not in your teeth. And there's no such word as qwertyuioplkjhgfdsa."

He was right—and I admitted it.

"I guess the Pepsodent people would like me to follow the copy a little closer," I said. "That's what you're telling me, isn't it?"

"Can't say," he said. "We're not their agency. I would imagine, though, they would want you to keep on doing whatever you're doing. You sure can sell products. It's not what you say. Could it be because you're a convincing guy?"

"That sounds nice," I said, "but I don't think I'm that good."

"You must be that good and that convincing," he grinned. "Until I went to the dictionary, you had me convinced that qwertyuioplkjhgfdsa was a word!"

Or, lady, to put it another way: sponsors and their agencies look upon me as a credibility gap.

This dumb book seems to be turning out just like the show: I kid agencies and sponsors both places. But let's keep the record straight. When these guys talk, I listen. And not because they're shelling out cash to keep us on the air. I listen because they are sincere and dedicated guys. When it comes to their products, they know whereof they speak. What they teach me I pass along to you. And because our show has only blue chip clients, which means I'm selling only topnotch items, I can believe in what I'm selling —and so can you. The three of us—client, agency man, and me—have only one purpose: to see that you get the best for your shopping dollar. I thank the good Lord that I can't sell a product I don't personally endorse. I may not be the greatest announcer and I may invent words like qwertyuioplkjhgfdsa, but when I tell you something about a product, ladies, you'd better believe it.

Why? Because *I* do. That's why.

I'll be honest, though. I have not personally tried every product we advertise. I have not tested Pampers. And as for the Gossard girdles and bras, I ain't the type. But I can know whereof I speak. Or, in the case of Gossard, I know whereof Marge, Colleen, Bonnie Lou, Marian, or you girls in the audience speak.

Example: Marge clued me on the wonders of En-dust. As she says: it doesn't leave any waxy film. Know why? Because there is no wax in it. *I* say En-dust don't leave no waxy film because it ain't got no wax in it. Marge doesn't say *ain't*.

Marge helps me all the time with my commercials. She's forever trying our clients' products. She goes crazy at Shillito's. But that's all right. If she were in

Dayton, she'd go crazy at Rike's. If she were in Indianapolis, she'd go crazy at L. S. Ayres. And if she were
in Columbus, she'd go crazy at Lazarus.

That's Marge for you: one crazy kid. But she had
to be crazy. What gal with good sense would marry
a dumbo like me?

The other day I explained to Bonnie Lou how Marge
went crazy at Shillito's—"She's got more stuff going
out and coming back than any five women in town,
Bonnie Lou. I keep asking her why she buys the stuff
when she knows she's not going to keep it. And she
keeps saying that she just wants to look at it. You
know how good Shillito's is at taking things back.
Listen, Marge bought a dress there four years ago—
and took it back yesterday. Shillito's has designated
one of their trucks as the Marge Dixon truck. Each
morning its driver stops by our house and says, 'Well,
here I am, lady. What goes back today?' And she loads
him up!"

Speaking of Shillito's—and *not* kidding this time—
may I say that I'm proud of my association with them?
Although department stores generally don't use as
much television advertising as they do newspaper advertising, Shillito's goes all out where our show is
concerned. But there have been moments when the
store wishes it hadn't. You've all seen Bonnie Lou,
Marian, and Colleen model the "dress of the day" from
Shillito's, haven't you? And you know the crazy low
prices on these one-day specials, don't you? Well,
every time we advertise a dress, the switchboard at
Shillito's is swamped with girls phoning in, wanting
that particular dress. We have sold as many as one
thousand dresses a day and, lady, that ain't hay.

"That Paul Baby can sell dresses all right," Shillito's Art Corston says, but if Art looks worried, he has good reason. He's the guy who got the idea that I could sell for Shillito's. Thanks to him, I'm where I am today. And thanks to me, he worries a lot. He can't forget the day I advertised a price lower than Shillito's had said. And the store lost a bundle on that goof of mine, but sell dresses they did! And at the price I advertised!

Art Corston, by the way, married Ivolou Ross who used to live in Cheviot, Ohio. He is now a vice president at Shillito's. Art worries most when I'm peddling Shillito's jewelry, because some of the pretties the store advertises on our show cost thousands of dollars. He's waiting for me to advertise the wrong price again. The other day I *did* show a ring which sold for $1500. I misread the price tag and said $15. Happily, I caught my error in time, but Gordy, in the control room, was having conniptions. What I'm saying is, Art Corston has reason to worry—and I have reason to be grateful to him.

Ivolou Corston, Art's wife, graduated from Western Hills High School. I thought I'd toss that in because it's one of the notes I made for this book and I can't find anywhere else that fact will fit.

Then there's Georgia Glynn, book buyer for Shillito's. She does more than buy books; she *makes* them happen. Mary Wood's book *Just Lucky I Guess* wouldn't have existed if Georgia hadn't pried it out of Mary. Georgia convinced Dick Perry that he should write *Vas You Ever in Zinzinnati?* She has done more to create Midwest literature than a dozen New York editors, but she does make a terrible mistake now and

then, like encouraging me to talk this book. Poor
Georgia. If her bosses find this out, chances are she'll
end up parking cars in the Shillito garage.

But where were we? Oh yes, talking about how
everyone worries when I do commercials.

Poor Gordy!

Only twenty-six years old and already he's hooked
on Upjohn Unicap Seniors. Producers age fast in control rooms—especially those sentenced to produce the
Dixon Show.

"Some day," Gordy once said, "you're going to surprise me and do a commercial straight from the copy."

"Do you think so?" I said hopefully.

He shook his head.

"No," he sighed. "I guess not. Like, the commercial
you did today for Vanish."

"What did I do wrong there?"

"I'm not sure," he said. "But Paul, I wonder if you
introduced the product right. Should you have said
what you did, about everyone going to the bathroom?
You made it come out right, but somehow . . ."

He looked sad.

"I wanted to show how Vanish gets bathrooms
clean," I said.

"And then there's Fiddle Faddle," Gordy went on.

"I thought I did a good job for them today," I said.

"Maybe so," he said, "but you introduced it by asking how many remembered the popcorn balls their
grandmothers used to make—and then by saying how
awful the grandmothers made popcorn balls."

"It's the truth," I said. "That's why Fiddle Faddle
is better."

"Shall we talk about Liquid Drano?" Gordy said.

"Do you have to start that commercial each morning by asking the audience if they have anything clogged up?"

"I *do* say that every time, don't I?" I said.

"And asking them how many had a bath that morning?" Gordy said.

"I don't know," I said. "But it sells Dove Beauty Soap. It's not a soap, you see. It's a combination of—"

"I know," muttered Gordy. "I know!"

Poor, poor Gordy! He has to put up with a lot. To make him feel better, I said: "Well, Gordy, there have been days when I did some pretty good commercials. I remember doing one last month that I thought was great."

"Why?" said Gordy.

"Because no one in the audience interrupted me during it," I said. "That's something, isn't it, Gordy? Though at the time, I worried. I thought they were dead."

And there Gordy went, down the corridor, muttering to himself.

Good old Gordy!

I'd be lost without Gordy.

And he knows it, too.

Which brings us up to a chapter about Gordy and the magicians who keep pulling my foot out of my mouth.

# 7.

## *Paul Baby &*

# GORDY'S MAGICIANS

☆ "Are remotes hard to do?"

One of you girls asked me that one day after the show. To those of you wondering what a "remote" is, I'd better explain fast. A remote is when we do our show from a location other than our studios. For instance, we have done Dixon Shows from Dayton, Columbus, and Indianapolis.

Remotes hard to do? They sure are. And the burden of their success falls on the shoulders of long-suffering Gordy and his long-suffering crew of magicians disguised as engineers, setup men, promotion men, office help, and thousands of others you at home never see. They do the real work. All I have to do is walk out on the stage and make a complete mess of their well-drawn schemes.

As Gordy once told me: "Paul, don't give me all the credit. We'd be lost without the help of our sister stations. Regardless of how much I seem to do, let's face it. The production, promotion, sales, and engineering staffs at WLW-I, WLW-C, and WLW-D do all the work on remotes."

So let this chapter sing the praises of Gordy and all the other unsung heroes who bend over backward to make me look better than I am.

Gordy is—of course!—Gordon Waltz, one of the finest producers I've been associated with; and I've been associated with some of the best in the business. Right now, though, I can see you looking at me thoughtfully, lady, and there's a question on your lips. The question is: "Does Gordy *really* drink?"

Lady, although I kid Gordy about drinking and sleeping in the control room, neither happens. Gordy has too many details to worry about to do either. The life of a television producer is not an easy one and, as I said, the life of the producer of our show is the saddest life of them all. Some who have produced the Dixon Show have moved on into the higher echelons of broadcast management. Lee Hornback is now an executive at WLW-Television. Still, to be honest, others have thrown up their hands after producing the Dixon Show and have got out of the business—*fast*. One became a meter reader for the waterworks. So I suppose it takes—and took—all kinds to produce our show. Of them all, Gordy is one of the most thoughtful and most efficient in his quiet and businesslike manner. Once, though, I heard him mutter: "Weeks

can go by and things will run smoothly with the
Dixon Show. Then, out of the blue, I can sit in the
control room and watch the show come apart at the
seams. I sit there as if my hands were tied. There's
nothing I can do but sit—and watch it happen!"

Gordy knows whereof he speaks when it comes to
producing shows. He is an old-timer around here. His
directing and producing days date back before television when WLW-Radio was "the cradle of the stars."
Gordy has sat in the control rooms of this place and
has seen the big names come and go. He has worked
with broadcast personalities who have more talent
than I ever hope to possess. Gordy remembers the old
WLW-Radio studios out on Arlington Street when
Red Skelton originated his first network show there.
And do you remember "Smoke Dreams"? Do you remember the "Armco Band"? Gordy was responsible
for those programs, too. Do you remember the "Boone
County Jamboree," which was the forerunner of the
"Midwest Hayride"? Gordy produced segments of that
show for the networks. But then came television—
and then came Dixon.

And there sits Gordy in the control room, becalmed!

Each television producer develops his own control
room style for giving directions to the cameramen,
sound man, switcher, floor men, and the rest. Years
ago Al Sternberg used to work with a combination of
shouts and screams and—at the strangest moments—
would laugh like there was no tomorrow. Lee Hornback was quiet, businesslike, and efficient. Len Goorian, during the rare moments he produced the show,
used to trade jokes with the floor man via the intercom. Abe Cowan would mutter in banana-boat

Spanish. Dick Perry called shots while making notes
for a novel.

And now there is Gordy. Neither a shouter nor a
laugher, when our show falls apart he calmly pulls it
back together again. So when he says that there's nothing he can do to "save" a show, Gordy is being modest.
Simply put, Gordy—and his magicians—are wonderful.

"Then why doesn't Gordy answer you when you ask
him a question?" you might be wondering.

Here's why: because he's in that control room doing
ten things at once. He's listening to me and also to a
host of others who are connected with the Dixon
Show. Perhaps he and the cameramen are setting up
a complicated sequence of shots. Perhaps audio engineer Lou Barnett is concerned about microphone
placements—and he and Gordy are hashing that out.
Perhaps the video switcher Charlie Guffin—he's the
engineer who punches buttons that change the picture from one camera to another—is pointing out
something. And, perhaps at the same time, Gordy
is engaged in a piecemeal conversation with the setup
crew out in the studio, via the intercom. And while
all this is going on at once, perhaps Gordy is talking
on the telephone to someone—who knows who! But
through it all Gordy sits calmly, carrying on a half-
dozen conversations at once, and quietly guides the
show from start to finish.

So why doesn't he answer me?

Lady, *that's* why!

I understand this—and he knows I understand this.
Can we help it, though, if we like to kid?

Come to think of it, I have not once seen Gordy

angry. If he gets angry—and many times he has
earned the right—he gets angry out of sight. I've never
once seen him brood. If he broods, he broods where
no one sees and is affected by it. When Gordy is with
me or with the engineers, talent, typists, musicians,
or setup men, he is the sweetest guy God ever made,
forever speaking in that soft voice, suggesting directions that make the Dixon Show better. But he refuses
to accept his own importance. Once he commented:
"Dixon knows what he's doing in front of the camera.
He doesn't need me to direct him. He has his job
and I have mine. Other than calling the shots during
the show and piecing it together technically in the
control room, my job is to see that Paul can do the
show without worrying about details. Do I get upset
if he complains about camera shots? No. He's kidding.
He kids the control room the same way he kids the
studio audience, Scratchy, or the band. Do engineers
get upset? Hardly ever. And when they do, their un-
happiness is fleeting. You see, to put on the Dixon
Show, each of us has his own area of responsibility.
The engineer at the console wants the best possible
sound. If there's good sound there, Lou Barnett will
find it. Charlie Guffin is interested in the smoothest
cuts between shots. And Paul is interested in the audience. My job is to gather these elements together—
and when you have a guy as talented as Dixon, and
engineers, each of whom is a perfectionist—my job
is a snap. Sometimes I think I could sit in the control
room and let the Dixon Show put itself together."

Wrong, Gordy! I'll be the first guy to disagree with
*that!* You are as essential to our show as I am and—
when I see all that you do—I think you are more es-

☆ On March 11, 1947, a building at Pearl and Race Streets collapsed, trapping a half-dozen employees. Rescuers dug a precarious tunnel to where they thought the trapped men were. And later, a microphone in my hand, I crawled through that same tunnel. Scared? You bet.

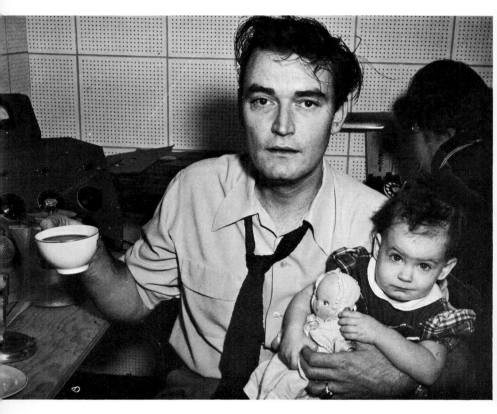

☆ When WCPO-Radio built a studio for me in the basement of our home, Pam would toddle into the studio, climb on my lap, yammer into the microphone, and—with equal abruptness—say "That's all."

☆ Somehow, by 9:00 or so, our studio is Kneesville.

☆ You might see John Franklin, Greg Moratschek, and Phil Rohrer (Scratchy) setting up the commercial props before the show.

☆ Famous movie stars have walked through the same double doors that you women come through each morning. Most of the great political figures of our time have come through those same doors, too. Among celebrated visitors, David McCallum and the late Senator Robert Kennedy.

☆ Why doesn't Gordy answer when I ask him a question? Here's why: because he's in that control room doing ten things at once.

☆ Frank Pierce, the weatherman, got into the act when he announced: "A big new front is moving in, followed closely by a big behind."

☆ Thanks to Bob Hope and John Murphy, Avco helped put together a crackerjack of a promotion for the Bob Hope Benefit Golf Match for Judge Benjamin Schwartz and Hope House in 1967. P.S. I beat both Murphy and Hope.

☆ Bruce Brownfield is as much a part of the show as
I am. Jerry Haggerty, who plays saxophone, is one of
the finest singers you'd ever want to meet. Marvin Cox,
the drummer, is a funny, *funny* guy. Larry Downing,
who plays bass, is a classic with that high voice version
of the Ink Spots. And Mel Horner on guitar is a comedian who comes up with the craziest lines.

sential. I know the engineers get fed up with me now and then. But, as you say, when that happens, their irritation comes and goes—fast. And you *are* right, Gordy. When they get irritated, they usually have good reason. I'm not the most professional critter they'll ever work with. I goof all the time.

And since I'm not sure what will happen, how can the poor cameramen know? They might be set up for a sequence of shots when suddenly—from the audience—a lady will sound off, and there you are. The planned shots go flying out the window. The engineers running the camera mutter and so does Lou Barnett on audio, as he twirls this knob and that, trying to find where the lady is. The cameramen who do the Dixon Show deserve medals. I'd be lost without them. The men are John Mitchell, Ed Gleason, Dave Wheeler, and Everett Winkle. The men on camera control—who "shade" the pictures—are Vern Madill, John Francis, Bob Thiele, and Walter Rogers. Long-suffering geniuses all!

They have to be geniuses because our show is not the easiest to do. I move around too much—and without notice. Sometimes I'll use this microphone, sometimes that one. This is bound to confuse Lou. And while I'm holding a dead microphone I may say something to him over the air. I'm certain that—under his breath—he's saying something back to me, but what he says we'll keep a control room secret; I'd rather not print that language in a book.

If you still think the crews at WLW-Television— be they in Cincinnati or any of the other Avco cities —are not the best, let me clue you, they *are*. Before I came back to WLW-Television I was on live from places like New York and Chicago. After we originated one show from WGN-TV in Chicago, an engineer there muttered: "Dixon, you don't have a show. You have an unscripted disaster."

The New York technicians were equally bewildered. Once we did our show from the now defunct Dumont Network in Manhattan. Our producer—of the Cincinnati school of television—wanted me to go outside onto the sidewalks with a camera and interview pedestrians. But the New York crew gave us ten thousand reasons why this was impossible.

First we would need special police permits to create the traffic jam. Second to move a camera from the studio to the sidewalk outside was an engineering impossibility. Third—and most important to them—it had never been done before.

"Well," I said to our producer, "I guess that kills that idea. But we could have done it in the Midwest."

"We can do it here, too," the producer said. "Wait and see."

So, during the show, the producer ordered a camera through the doors and out to the sidewalk. The cameraman—surprised—did as he was told. No one had told him it couldn't be done. Once the camera was positioned on the sidewalk, the producer motioned me outside, and there you are!

We created a whopper of a traffic jam, as the program director had predicted. I guess it doesn't take much to attract a crowd in New York, does it?

Afterward, the New York program director gave me a look of despair and muttered the Brooklynese equivalent of: "What's a mother to do!"

But as I mumbled at the start of this chapter, remotes ain't fun for Gordy. To do our show from the

Cincinnati studios under normal conditions is hectic
enough. Plunk us into an auditorium away from home
base and—mercy! You should see the details that
Gordy and the others iron out before I can say hello to
you from Dayton, Indianapolis, or Columbus.

First, Gordy has to make sure that I'm *there*. Sounds
simple, doesn't it, but guess again. Once, at the Ohio
State Fair, I almost was not allowed into the Grandstand to do my show. The guard blocked my path
with a friendly—but firm—comment of: "Sorry, mister. You can't go busting in there. Don't you know
there's a television show about to start?"

"I know," I said, "because I'm in it. It *is* the Paul
Dixon Show, isn't it?"

"Right," he said. "But if you got no ticket you can't
go in."

"But I have to," I stammered. "I'm Paul Dixon."

"Now I heard everything, mister," he said. "All I
know is, if you got no ticket, you don't get in."

I had stupidly forgotten to wear the badge that the
Columbus crew had provided for me. Happily, a member of the band identified me, and I managed to sneak
in to my own show. So you see Gordy's problem: if
anyone goofs, that person will be me. The fact that
I had forgotten the badge wasn't his fault, was it?
I'm a grown-up person. I should be able to think a
little for myself!

"Sorry, Gordy," I say—honestly—each time I've
committed another goof.

"Think nothing of it, Paul," he will say. "We all
make mistakes."

That's Gordy for you! Kind, efficient—and for-
giving.

What makes Gordy—and his magicians—old before

their time? Consider the details that had to be handled when we moved our show to Dayton, Ohio, in October, 1967. We did the remote from Memorial Hall, remember? Well, first Gordy had to console me. You see, no matter how often you inundate us with ticket requests, I feel the next time the bubble will break—and on our next remote, not a soul will show up. So that Dayton remote was no different. Gordy told me not to worry, but I worried anyway. Walter Bartlett, the vice president in charge of all our television stations, told me not to worry. I worried nonetheless. Don Dahlman, the general manager at WLW-D, told me not to worry. So did George Resing, the WLW-D program director. Scratchy told me not to worry and Jack Donahue the WLW-D promotion manager told me not to worry. Greg told me not to worry—and then he asked for an increase in his allowance. Well, to make a long worry short, I stopped worrying only when Bill McCluskey told me 25,000 tickets had been requested. I stopped worrying about that—and began to worry about something else.

"Suppose the weather turns bad, Gordy?" I said.

"I can't do anything about the weather," Gordy sighed. "Just don't worry. Didn't they show up at Indianapolis during a blizzard?"

"I guess you're right," I said and stopped worrying —for ten minutes. After he left, though, I started again. A blizzard was one thing, but what about a cloudburst? None had been predicted, not even rain, but that's the way I am. But each time, I worry needlessly. You women are as dependable as the U.S. mail: neither rain nor sleet, nor . . . a whole lot of real heavy rain . . . nor . . . I forget how it goes, but you know what I mean. You always show up.

You're great—and so are Gordy and his magicians. Once they think I've stopped worrying (but you and I know that I haven't, don't we?) they can worry about the details each remote creates. And listen to the variety:

Who makes sure that your tickets are mailed and that those who don't get tickets do get regrets? Gordy and Jack Donahue, the WLW-D promotion manager in Dayton. In Columbus it's Gordy and WLW-C's promotion manager Rod Warner. In Indianapolis, it's Gordy and WLW-I's promotion manager Stan Pederson. Who makes certain the salami award winner (that poor—or *lucky*—soul whose name was next after all the tickets had been mailed) gets her salami? Gordy—and George Resing the WLW-D program director in Dayton; Jack Donahue has a hand in it too, for Dayton. In Columbus Gordy and Rod Warner and Dick Thrall do that chore; in Indianapolis Gordy and Stan Pederson. Who makes sure the motorcade can find the house where the salami winner lives? Gordy —and the promotion manager from whichever city we're doing the remote from.

Gordy and his magicians in Dayton made sure there were display signs at Dayton's Memorial Hall. Jack Donahue even spelled out the *size* of the signs: three feet by forty feet! About the only thing Gordy and WLW-Television leave to chance is me. And even so, they make sure that I don't get lost. They plunk me into the middle of a motorcade, organized by Donahue, and away I go, following a motorcycle policeman, arranged for by Donahue.

Details, details, details—but Gordy's magicians are taking care of every one. Example: when we do a remote, we arrive at the city the night before. Do we

sleep on park benches? Nope. Thanks to Gordy and
the sister stations, we have hotel reservations. For the
Dayton remote described here, WLW-D reserved a
dozen rooms for us visiting firemen—and, afterward,
made sure the bills were paid. At the hotel WLW-D
arranged for two large signs to hang over the hotel
entrance.

WLW-D Welcomes the Paul Dixon Show

*and*

Paul Dixon Sleeps Here, October 5, 1967

I think that was carrying things a bit too far, I'm
not that famous, but the point is WLW-D went all out.
You should have seen the breakfast menus the next
morning:

Paul baby's breakfast!
    Outlandish orange juice
    Two farm-fresh eggs looking right at you!
    Side order of salami (disguised as ham, sau-
        sage, or bacon)
    Bonnie lou's burnt buttered toast
    Marge's magnificent marmalade
    Colleen's craazzzyyy coffee
Breakfast definitely not served by a
    dumb waiter!

Gordy—and WLW-D—arranged for us to visit the
Wright-Patterson Air Force Base Hospital while we
were in Dayton that year. Donahue and Resing made
the arrangements with the hospital commander, Colo-
nel Hennessen, and the public relations specialist
Dave Larrimore. We presented to one of the wards
a portable color television which bore the sign:

> If this set is not tuned to Paul Dixon's Show Monday
> through Friday from 9 to 10 A.M., all military per-
> sonnel within 20 feet of this set will have active duty
> extended six months.

Some of the patients I met were soldiers who had
been injured in Vietnam. No matter *how* you feel
about the war itself, it tears your heart out to see these
guys. Even though some of them looked like they
should still have been in school, they are brave, brave
men. I was awed. I was impressed. I felt I was visiting men who, although unable to stand, were standing ten feet tall. So you can see that Gordy and the
staffs at our sister stations have hearts, too. They
had arranged the hospital visit for me. I thank the
Lord they did.

In Dayton, in addition to all the other arrangings,
WLW-D arranged a cocktail party for clients and
members of the press. They ordered the food, arranged
for the hall, the works! Gordy and the crew also saw
to it everyone had an invitation to come—and an iden-
tification badge when he got there. Also, they arranged
for parking space. And later that day, as if they hadn't
arranged enough, they set up a dinner party for sixteen! And on and on and on. Can you see, lady, why
Gordy has little time to answer me on the air? He
hardly has time to call home and talk with his family!

And who else but Gordy—with ten thousand other
things on his mind—would make sure the floor crew
and the engineers had breakfast before the remote?
Since everyone had to be at the auditorium before
the show started, Gordy had food there, ready and
waiting when they walked through the doors. Who
arranged for the Dayton mayor—David Hall—to make
it Dixon Day in Dayton? One of the WLW-D magi-

cians! Gordy, before going on a remote, does his homework well. Before going to Dayton he was reading reports like this, going into detail about the salami
award winner—

". . . the house is worth mentioning. It is baby blue.
It has blue awnings across the front, sits on a hill,
and has a loveseat on the porch. Mrs. Fritz has a color
television, is active in school affairs, and says she'll get
everybody from school to her house to meet Paul
Baby . . ."

Also, Gordy and his magicians handle technical
aspects of remotes. Arrangements had to be made to
"feed" the Dixon Show to Cincinnati from Memorial
Hall in Dayton; then, from Cincinnati, back again
out over the four-station network. Crazy as it sounds,
the picture you Dayton viewers saw had traveled to
Cincinnati and back before being transmitted out
from a tower! Gordy and the engineers made those
arrangements with the telephone company. Engineers
on remotes are great, too. They work round the clock
installing equipment—for a one-night stand!

In Dayton, the engineering magicians are led by
Robert Wehrman. His crew includes Fred Stone,
Joseph Bell, Don Kuykendall, Tony Pajnic, James
Carlton, and Charles Weiss. In Indianapolis the en-
gineering staff is led by Norman Nixon. His crew is
Jerry Blankenbeker, Charles McQuigg, Leo Klinger,
Frank Hull, John Zuber, Charles Swearingen, and Bill
Sanders. The Columbus chief engineer is Bob Dye. His
crew is Russ Tracy, Mel Metzmaier, Clete Johnson,
Jack Pritchard, Chuck Lutz, Randy Clum, Bill James,
Dick McCarley.

Maybe you shouldn't run a bunch of names in a

book like this. The way I feel is, these guys belong in my book because they deserve public thanks. Without them there'd be no book because there would be no Dixon Show. Now that their neighbors will know who they work with, they'll probably have to move out of their neighborhoods.

But back to the details of doing just that one Dayton remote—and you'll see what we go through for each one. Arrangements were made with the American Federation of Musicians so Bruce Brownfield and his boys could play in Dayton. Parking permits were needed at Memorial Hall. Prizes had to be obtained before they could be given out to you. Eight policemen were needed for special duty, plus flowers for the stage. Tuning the piano? Union stagehands?

And, this happens every remote!

Also, a television program needs cameras, lights, microphones, chewing gum, nails, stage braces, saws, and hammers. When we travel our show—which is "show talk" for taking our show to another location, but I used "travel our show" to save a little time, only I guess I didn't save too much, did I? Anyway, as I started to say, when we travel our show (see explanation above!) Gordy oversees all the odds and ends. For instance, in Dayton, Bob Wehrman and his engineers had to install a control room in the orchestra pit at Memorial Hall. But Gordy had to make sure, along with Bob Wehrman, that cameras were placed to proper advantage. Gordy arranged with Bob Wehrman for eight different microphones and a place to store Colleen's marimba! Gordy and Bob made sure we had television monitors—those television sets on which we can watch the show fall apart. Gordy scheduled the setup crew. Gordy scheduled the commercial props. Gordy and his magicians did everything, in fact, but jump in front of the camera and tell the studio audience how beautiful they were!

So let this chapter be a tribute to the unsung magicians who toil behind the scenes. As for Gordy, lady—well, Gordy is good. He doesn't need me. But I've got news for you. I need him—and I ain't just whistling "Dixie" when I say that. *Why* ain't I whistling "Dixie"? Only because Gordy hasn't cleared the music. That's why.

What do *I* do on remotes if everyone else does all the work? Lady, I thought you'd never ask.

# 8.

# *Paul Baby &*

# COLUMBUS

☆ "What do you do—and think about—when you do a show from another city?"

As I said, lady, I thought you'd never ask, but I do get asked that by the studio audience at least once a week. The question is easy to answer. In the last chapter we talked about Dayton. Now let's see what I do on a Columbus remote—for instance, the one in February, 1968, from the Veterans Memorial Auditorium there. What do I think about?

Well, I think about everything but the kitchen sink —and sometimes I think about that, too.

You see, there's more to "doing" a show from another city than clomping on the stage and having fun with you in the audience. In the last chapter, I showed you the things that Gordy our producer has to think about during a remote. Let me take you along with me, hour by hour, in this chapter, and show you what I think about, worry about, have fun with, and —and well, everything!

First, I have to think about getting to Columbus. That seems simple enough, doesn't it? We did the Columbus show on a Friday. But on Thursday, the day before, Marge and I took off like birds as soon as the Thursday show was over in Cincinnati. She drove. Zoom! Why did she drive? I was pooped. So the minute I got in the car I shut my eyes tight. I didn't open them until we pulled up at our Columbus hotel. I always close my eyes when I'm in the car and Marge is driving. I close my eyes and pray a lot. When the others on the interstate see Marge behind the wheel they pray a lot, too. Oh, she's a good driver. What mother isn't? But she makes up rules as she goes along. She invents traffic patterns. She is so busy looking out the rear mirror for police that she never looks through the windshield. That's why I pray. To ride with Marge driving is a religious experience.

Anyway, I opened my eyes in Columbus.

Bruce Brownfield had already arrived. And so had Colleen Sharp and Alice Rastani, my Girl Friday. The hotel lobby was crowded with personnel from WLW-C, plus photographers shooting pictures of my entrance. The first thing everyone shouted was: "Paul Baby, go out and come in again!"

It seems I had barged into the lobby before they had their cameras focused. I came in three times for three different pictures. Each time I was greeted—in the film—by someone else. I would have come in the fourth time but Marge tugged at my sleeve, grinned, and pointed at my cardigan sweater.

"Cops!" I said. I had either buttoned wrong, or the sweater had one buttonhole too many at the top and one button too many at the bottom. So that's what the Columbus viewers saw on WLW-C that night; me with egg on my face and Marge grinning. I'd be lost without Marge.

It was 2:30 Thursday afternoon. Now you'd suppose we'd take life easy for the rest of the day, to be bright-eyed and bushy-tailed for the show the next day. Well, don't suppose that or you will have supposed wrong, lady. Marge and I hardly had time to get up to our room before the telephone rang and Rod Warner, the promotion man for WLW-C was saying: "Okay, Paul Baby. We're ready to shove off for Lockbourne!"

And there I was: back downstairs again and into a car, heading to Lockbourne Air Force Base with Bruce, Colleen, Bonnie, and others. We were to present a color television set to the 121st Tactical Fighter Group of the Ohio National Guard. This bunch had been called to active duty only a week or so before.

As we drove to the base, I looked at Colleen and said: "What have you got in the paper sack?"

"My lunch," she sighed. "I'm starved. And we haven't had time to eat."

Now there's what I call a real down-to-earth living doll. Who else would ride in a $22,471.34 Mercedes-Benz 600—and eat a $1.10 sack lunch! Well, that's what I always say: you can take a girl out of Economy (Indiana) but you can't take Economy (Indiana) out of a girl. No wonder Indians love her! The rest of us love her, too!

When we got to the air base, we ran into tragedy.

*Real* tragedy. It seems that while Marge and I were driving to Columbus one of the planes of the 121st Tactical Fighter Group had plunged to earth in central Indiana, killing its pilot. As I walked into the headquarters building I could sense the heartbreak that filled the corridors. The officers and men tried to put on a good face for us, but you could see the pain in their eyes. Talk about bringing the war close to home! It tears me up even now to recall that afternoon at the base. All I could think of, when they told me what had happened, was: "Oh God . . . oh God!"

Plans had been made for a presentation of the color television. Colleen and Bonnie were going to sing, Bruce was going to play, and I was going to clown a little, but common decency told us to scrap those plans. We were in no mood for that kind of stuff and certainly the men there were not. Instead we made a simple presentation in an office—and left quietly.

As we drove out of the base I couldn't help but feel the loneliness that those men back there were feeling. But this isn't the kind of stuff I talk about on the show, is it? When we're on the air, our job is to entertain. Period. Yet, on the ride back into Columbus from the air force base I felt a nagging sadness. As I said elsewhere in this book, how you or I feel about the Vietnam situation is not the stuff my show is made of. But it's the stuff our country is made of, isn't it? I looked at Colleen and Bonnie and they looked at me. We didn't have to say anything. We understood. We had left a part of our hearts back there—with those brave men.

And with their wives, their mothers, and—what tears you up—their children.

Our schedule was too fast-paced for us to belabor the sadness we felt. We stepped out of the car at the hotel and stepped into the middle of a serenade by some of the prettiest college girls God ever put on this earth: members of the Theta Phi Alpha Sorority from Ohio University, in Athens, Ohio. That's Pam's sorority but not her college. Pam attends the University of Cincinnati; but her sorority sisters made us feel extra welcome in Columbus. Great girls—every single one of them!

What do I *think* about as Marge and I stand on the hotel stairs listening to these young ladies sing? Well, first you're pleased with the girls. They seem so fresh and nice and well-mannered. You think—fleetingly— that here are young people who will never make ugly headlines and you think—gratefully—that most young kids you've met are really nice. It's just the few who cause the rest to get the ugly names we attach too quickly to all.

Then you think about Rod Warner—and the others of the WLW-C staff. You know that before you entered the lobby, the WLW-C crew got with these girls, helped them stage themselves so they would look good for the newsreel cameras, and you feel humble. You really do. And you stand on the stairs, listening to the girls sing, and you know you don't deserve any of this. But there they are.

And other thoughts—different but important— plague you. Tomorrow's show. Will Colleen's marimba be set up in time? Will anyone show up—or will the auditorium be empty? You think about the prizes to be awarded: are they there? You think about the audio in that auditorium: feedback, or what? Suppose one

of the cameras goes out? Or all three of them? You
stand, listen to the girls sing, and you think about
a thousand things. You know that Gordy and the crew
have taken care of all the details about audio, cameras, and everything, but you stand there, listening to
the girls sing, and your stomach is filled with butterflies.

> *On this special day,*
> *The girls of Theta Phi come your way . . .*

They serenade you—and you've never been sere-
naded before. Marge is beside you and you're glad that
she's there. You only wish that Pam and Greg could be
with you, too. These thoughts race through your
mind. And in between these thoughts you remember
the faces of the men you met at the air force base and
the loss you saw in their eyes.

> *. . . So the girls of Theta Phi*
> *Wish to give a "hi"*
> *To a special guy.*

You search the crowd gathered in the lobby and see
the smiling face of Bill McCluskey. He winks—and
you feel better. For one brief moment—and one brief
moment only—you relax and listen to the girls sing.
Their singing is beautiful, beautiful. . . .

Suppose the weather turns bad? Suppose no one
shows up at the auditorium? Your moment of relaxation is gone, lady. It's gone like it was never there
at all. Bill McCluskey smiles at you, but it's no use.
Sorry, Bill. You know because you're a show business
professional. You know there are times when a reassurance doesn't reassure.

Thirty minutes later you are in the Top of the Center Restaurant, one of the city's finest. But no relaxation here. You feel the butterflies in your stomach. You make smalltalk with Bruce's wife Mildred. Marge is at your side. You look at her, she looks at you, and you know she understands what you're going through. Members of the Columbus press arrive, you greet them gratefully because they've been good to you, and soon you are lost in conversation with them. You chat with Jo Bradley Reed who had written in the *Citizen-Journal:*

> "How do I get a couple of tickets to the Paul Dixon Show at Veterans Memorial Friday?" This is the question we have been answering all week.
>
> All tickets (4,000) for Paul's show have long been distributed on a first come, first served basis since he announced the middle of January he was bringing his show to Columbus for the first time (outside of his Ohio State Fair appearance last fall).

Soon you are seated at a long table, food comes, but you have little time to eat. In another half hour you are whisked away—no time for dessert—to a hotel where the Ohio Chamber of Commerce is holding a dinner. Bonnie, Colleen, Bruce, and others are with you as you enter the dining room where the chamber holds its banquet. You have no time to meet anyone. You are guided quickly to the speakers' table and introduced. You stand there, tired and worried, as you are presented with a plaque which names you Man of the Year for the promotion job of Kneesville, U.S.A.

You say words of thanks. Some of your words are funny. Some are serious. The audience seems to like you. Mostly men. And few get a chance to watch your show. You had entered that room worried sick: how could they possibly like you when they've never seen you? You leave the room—and you feel awed. For some reason they liked you. They actually *liked* you!

The hour is late as you and the rest wait outside the hotel for taxis to carry you back to your own hotel. Bonnie laughs with Colleen about something. Rod Warner is waving at taxis. The photographers struggle with their gear. But you stand by yourself and feel the bite of the air. Cold. Real cold. You sniff. There's a hint of snow in the air. Suppose the weather turns bad? Suppose no one shows up? . . .

Later, after the rest have settled in their rooms to sleep, you sit on the edge of your bed too tired to undress. A weather report is coming up on television. You turn the set off. You don't want to know about the weather. Our show easy to do? Not then, lady, not then. You sit in an unfamiliar hotel room and die a thousand deaths from a thousand worries while the city is sound asleep. This is a side of Dixon I don't show on the air. But Marge knows it. And now, so do you. If I were *good* at this business of entertaining, things would be different. But I'm not good. I'm only lucky.

So I worry about everything, like the possibility of snow and the placement of Colleen's marimba—*if* it doesn't get lost in transit. I worry long after Marge is breathing the steady breathing of sleep. I stare at the ceiling and, in my mind, I do the show over and over and over.

Just before I do fall asleep, I think of that plane falling from the sky and I think of the loneliness of the men I saw today, the loneliness of men still alive.

And what do you think about on the day of the show? First, you think about the weather. Marge wakes you up, you look out the hotel window, and you feel better. The sun is *actually* shining. No blizzard or sleet like in Indianapolis. You shave, shower, and look out the window again. Snowflakes. And a howling wind! Your Dixon luck holds true: bad weather on every remote. Sunshine might follow some guys; why can't it follow you? As you eat breakfast you refuse to look out the window again. You know what you will see: miserable weather.

Suppose the weather turns so bad that no one shows up?

You make jokes with Marge. But, inside and out of sight, you don't feel like joking. Those butterflies again. Where was that golden-voiced theatrical ham who said that some day you would get used to doing a show? He probably went broke, betting on the horses. Mercy!

By eight, you are on your way—through the darned bad weather, of course—to the auditorium. You know that others have been there before you. Bob Dye, WLW-C chief engineer, has been on the scene since before six. So have the stagehands. And when Bob and the stagehands arrived, they found that even they were not first. Huddled in the dark and cold doorway of the auditorium were two women, shivering. They were not able to hide themselves from the elements that froze their fingers. They shivered in that doorway until the doors opened at eight. That's how much they wanted to be first!

For me, you wonder? They stood in the dark and cold for me?

Your heart goes out to them—and to all the other earlybirds. You are told that by 7:30 the doorway to the auditorium was a press of shivering people unable to avoid the wind, but unwilling to sit in their cars. They were waiting to see you. You shake your head in amazement. You are bewildered—and grateful. You're not that good and you know it. To say they shouldn't have stood there in the cold sounds trite, but that is exactly what you feel. They shouldn't have done it. You know you'll have to work even harder to entertain them. They deserve only the best because they are great—but all you have to give them is you.

"All they're getting is our show," you sigh. If you could you would give them the sun and the moon, but the sun and the moon are not yours to give. You can only give them laughter. You can't give them greatness, you can only give them a salami.

These are the things you think about as you mill around backstage where, it seems to you, hundreds of others are milling restlessly, too. You arrived at 8:15 but you know Bruce Brownfield and the musicians have been at the auditorium since 7:15. And the prop boys—along with Scratchy—were there long before that. Colleen and Bonnie were there before you, too. They had run through their songs by 7:45. And Bill McCluskey was early, being everywhere in the auditorium at the same time, checking this and checking that, like a wise and wonderful mother hen. Gordy has checked ten thousand details—and has finished the check by the time you arrive. So, when you walk in, all the last-minute checking is completed. There is nothing to do but wait.

And waiting—lady, *that* is the hardest part!

The audience has yet to be admitted to the auditorium—and on the stage are two dozen people: stagehands, engineers, prop boys, Colleen, Bonnie, Bruce, the band! A traffic jam. Backstage—in the wings—is the same, or worse. It seems as if a hundred Boy Scouts have assembled to present their annual report to Governor Rhodes on our show. And it seems that each scout has parents with him. Crowded, crowded, crowded. With butterflies in your stomach, you wander amid the backstage horde. You stop and talk with Bruce's wife. You move on, stopping to talk with Bill McCluskey, and—still nervous—you move on again, pacing, looking, wondering, worrying.

Marge looks at you from across the crowd. She grins, you grin back, and that makes you feel a little better.

But not much—and Marge knows it. She has seen you go through this torment each time you do a remote. And, back at the station itself, she has seen you go through this same torment each time you do a show. You know, of course, that the minute you step out on the stage, your fears will go away. But knowing that does not console you.

Suppose *this* time is different?

So you worry, pace, make nervous conversation, and half the time you can't remember the face of the person you're talking to—or what you're even talking about.

A different noise now. You recognize it instantly. The auditorium doors have been opened, the audience is filling the seats. They murmur as they enter, that first trickle of people, but soon the trickle becomes a flood, a torrent of women, and the noise grows greater and greater. Before they entered, their murmur was muffled by the closed door of the auditorium. Now that buffer is gone; the noise goes into the very heart of your being as you stand in the wings knowing that it's for you. And in what seems like only moments, the empty auditorium is filled— every seat, upstairs and down, *over four thousand people!* You peep out. The weather didn't stop them. This becomes a phrase you repeat over and over to yourself like a child's rhyme: the weather didn't stop them, the weather didn't stop them. . . .

*Every seat occupied!*

You hear later that when Scratchy stood out there in the lobby, watching the people come through the doors, most of them would look over and say: "Hey, there's Scratchy!"

Or: "Hi, Scratchy!"

Or: "Scratchy, please. May I have your autograph?"

But now it's only minutes from airtime—and they're all in the auditorium. A stream of ladies comes forward to the stage, bringing gifts. They climb the steps to the stage, go to the desk where Colleen and Bonnie are, and the two girls accept each gift with cheery grins and polite thank-you's. The girls sit, accepting gifts, while the image of them appears in the black-and-white television monitors because the cameramen are checking camera focus for the last time before the show.

You grin from the wings. Those engineers aren't fools. They'd rather take pictures of Bonnie and Colleen instead of a test pattern any old day.

And you don't blame them one bit!

A stagehand passes near you.

"Where's Colleen's marimba?" you ask.

He shrugs.

Doesn't know.

Details, details, details. And always—somewhere!
—there's a snag. It is one minute before airtime.
The announcer is on stage, warming up the audience.
Colleen and Bonnie are out there, too, helping. But
you listen backstage and—out of the corner of your
eye—you see Colleen's marimba arrive—in the nick
of time. That, you think, was much too close! And
you fret, "What are they trying to do to me!" You
chew your gum faster now and stand by yourself,
waiting, waiting, waiting. The band is introduced and
settled in their bandstand, waiting, waiting, waiting.

Gordy is at your side, muttering last-minute
reminders; you nod, but you don't hear a word he
says. Part of you hears, but not the part that stands
there, trapped in a storm of butterflies.

The longest minute in the world.

Waiting, waiting, waiting.

Bonnie is on the stage, saying: "We're so happy
to be here with all you lovely ladies in this part
of Ohio . . ."

The audience murmurs approval; they love Bonnie, too.

Waiting, waiting, waiting.

You peer out at the audience again. More butterflies. Someone is standing beside you, telling about
the traffic jam that your Dixon Show has created
on the streets of Columbus. Even the mayor, Maynard
E. Sensenbrenner, they tell you, had to get out and
walk to the auditorium! You look about. Governor

Rhodes has arrived—with his two grandchildren in tow. As you hurry through the crowd backstage to say hello to him, a stagehand taps your arm.

"Sorry," he murmurs. "No smoking backstage."

As you talk with the governor a silence falls over the crowd backstage as well as the women in the auditorium. The silence is almost electric in its power. Then you hear Marvin Cox give the opening on the drum and the announcer saying: "Live . . . and in color . . . from Veterans Memorial Auditorium . . . in Columbus . . . it's the . . . PAUL . . . DIXON . . . SHOW!"

The band sings the introduction. Then Bonnie shouts to the audience: "And now, here he is: the one . . . the only . . . Paul Baby!"

You crush out your cigarette, straighten your shoulders, and go—almost at a trot—out onto that stage. The noise of the audience pours over you like warm water. You mug. They react. They laugh. You laugh. And the butterflies? What butterflies, lady? You're home again—*among friends.* And you proceed to do the same show you do every day.

It's as simple as that!

Later that day you will visit the home of the Columbus salami award winner. And later that day you will go to Worthington, Ohio, to run an actual railroad train. "You run your railroad, I'll run mine," you'll shout out the cab of the engine as it toots along the track. Then there will be a lunch at the Jai Lai, and then that trip back down the interstate, with Marge driving. Much awaits, but let it wait. You have to do a show for an auditorium filled with your friends. During the band's first number you think for a moment of the plane that fell from the sky the day before. The loneliness returns—briefly. You decide you cannot speak of that matter no matter how much it tears your heart.

No, your job is to make the people out there have— for ninety minutes at least—a little happiness. Let others talk of death. You are the court jester. So what do I think about during a remote, lady? As I said before, I think about everything but the kitchen sink.

And at times, I think of death and loneliness— because I am human, too.

# 9.

## *Paul Baby &*

## A TYPICAL DAY

☆ "What a racket you have, Paul Baby. Other men work eight hours a day. You work an hour and a half—and you are through. You've got a snap, haven't you?"

It seems that way, doesn't it? And I'll be the first to admit that what I do is fun. I get a kick out of doing the Dixon Show.

But do I work *only* an hour and a half a day?

And am I through after that?

Lady, if I did work only that long each day, I would be through. Period. I wouldn't have a show! And that is the unvarnished truth. In fact, the easiest part of my day is when I *am* on the air.

130

Look at a typical Dixon day—and then, decide for yourself.

First of all, I'm up each weekday morning at 6:00. I don't leave the house until around 7:30 but some men are fast starters in the morning and others are slow starters. Call me the slowest starter of them all. I spend ten minutes looking into the bathroom mirror, trying to wake up enough to shave. Imagine having to stare at *me* at that awful hour! It ain't easy, lady. I even hate to look at myself on the monitor when we're on the air.

Well, I spend ten minutes more—yawning, stretching, scratching, taking a shower, and wondering what day it is. Did I say I was the slowest starter? I could win prizes for standing still! There have been mornings when I sit at the breakfast table and stare for minutes. What do I stare at? I can't remember. After you have looked at a face like mine in the mirror, you tend to spend the rest of the morning a little shaken.

Somehow or other, my breakfast is prepared. I suppose Marge prepares it. I am too busy staring, yawning, stretching, scratching and wishing I was back in bed. My usual breakfast? Black coffee. And cereal. That's all. Oh, I'd love to eat a good old-fashioned country breakfast of pancakes by the stack, fried eggs, bacon, biscuits, gobs of melted butter— *or* margarine—and gallons of syrup. Can't do that, though. I stick with black coffee and cereal. Otherwise I'd be as big as Jackie Gleason. I could never step into that artist's shoes, but unless I watch my weight carefully I could easily step into one of his suits!

By 7:30 I'm wide awake which is a good thing for
highway safety because I'm driving in the rush-hour
traffic along Columbia Parkway. In New York, I com-
muted by train. Give me Columbia Parkway any old
day. At least in the Midwest, when you drive, you
drive. Once when we lived in New York I drove in
from the suburbs to Manhattan—and spent most of
the time wedged in bumper-to-bumper traffic that
didn't move.

Sometimes on the way to the WLW-Television studios here in Cincinnati, I'll see someone in the car
next to me look surprised that I'm driving my own
car. They'll wave like crazy. Why is that? Do they
think I come to work each morning on a broom?
Heavens no. I leave the broom in the garage. Marge
uses it for shopping trips. Actually, not too many
wave at me on Columbia Parkway in the morning.
Only a woman may know what another wants at nine
o'clock in the morning, but if she's tooling along Columbia Parkway all she wants is a clear lane.

And so I pull into the parking lot across the street
from the studios and park in my usual spot. Moments
later I am hurrying down the hall to my office—and
as usual I'm whistling. Alice Rastani, my Girl Friday
and the cutie you see demonstrating that Niagara
chair or opening the doors of a Shillito refrigerator,
says I've yet to miss a morning when I whistle my
way down the hall.

"And always a happy tune," she mutters.

Girl Fridays ain't too cheerful at that hour, but
can I help it if I'm a natural-born whistler? Almost
got tossed out of a hotel in Cologne, Germany, because I whistle. Greg and I walked into the hotel lobby,

I was whistling to beat the band, and an angry gentleman trotted up to me, glared, and said something in German about my whistling.

"Zxcvbnmlkjhgfdsaqwertyuiop!!!" he raged—or words to that effect. I don't understand German too well. And my English isn't too good, either.

Had trouble in Rome, too. Wanted to do as the Italians did, and pinch women. Women just frowned at me. They didn't giggle the way they giggled when they were pinched by Italians.

Colleen Sharp figured out why.

So did Bonnie.

"I guess," they said, "they could tell you were from out of town."

So much for my foreign travels—and back to my working day. Well, there I am in my office. On the desk is a fresh stick of chewing gum, placed there each morning by Alice, who knows me like a book, but not this one. I rescued Alice from the Uncle Al program where she had done a five-year term of keeping an eye on the babies. She looks upon the rescue with mixed emotions. She gave up handling fifty small babies a day to handle one big one! Imagine five years of fifty babies a day! And they say Cincinnati isn't where the action is. Mercy!

I spend fifteen or twenty minutes at my desk before the show, going through the folder which contains the program material I'll use that day: letters from you women, fact sheets for commercials, and odd scraps of papers on which I've scribbled notes that I can't read. This folder is our script. You didn't know I used a script, did you? I have the only script in television that contains chewing gum wrappers.

By 8:10—at the latest—I'm padding about the studio itself. The audience has yet to come up from the lobby. I talk with Gordy and check things with him. I talk with Scratchy and check things with him. I check things with Alice, I check things with members of the band, and I check things with the engineers. I check things with anyone, even the delivery man. The trouble is, there's nothing to check.

Gordy, Bruce, and the others are too efficient. I could arrive at the studio ten minutes before we go on the air, and things would run just as smoothly. In fact, they might run even smoother. But I'm a worrier. I have to make sure the commercial props are where I know they are anyway—and I have to make sure the band is scheduled to play the selections they are already scheduled to play. I have to check the cameramen to see that the cameras are working. So I spend my time getting in everyone's way, bothering everyone, but I'm checking. I whistle—and I check.

And I worry. I'm the only guy I know who can— at the same time—whistle, check, and worry.

And I chew my gum like crazy.

Have you ever tried whistling, checking, worrying, *and* chewing gum, lady? It ain't easy.

The women come into the studio around 8:30, and I clear out. It's not that I'm a star. It's just that Bruce, the band, and I hide until you women get seated. Promptly at 8:50, though, I walk into the studio and that, lady, is when I start to put together the Dixon Show: ten minutes before we go on the air!

Of course, for a performer to be seen by the audience *before* he officially starts is against every rule of "show business." A New York advertising man expressed surprise that I went out into a studio to talk with the girls in the audience before the show, and that I actually did my own "warmup."

"Paul," he said, "that's not the way things are done. Stay in the wings until the last moment and then go out, after a big introduction."

He is probably right—I'll admit I've much to learn —but let me explain why I go out before the show starts at 9:00, and you tell me what you think. My point is, our Dixon Show isn't like any other. Not that it's greater or better, but it's different. The women in our studio audience each day are, in my opinion, as much a part of the Dixon Show as I am. So I go out and chat with them. Does that make sense?

Suppose one of you girls is wonderfully gabby during the warmup. Suppose you come out with some gems. Well, I've made a mental note to get back to you once we're on the air. Also, during the warmup is when I see how many of you are pregnant—"on the nest," as we say. I find out all kinds of things. You'd be surprised what you tell me in those ten minutes before we hit the air. This girl wants to play the piano. A lady up there wants to say hello to eight billion relatives. That man in the aisle—three rows back— has a whopper to tell about Partridge Whoppers. The woman by the railing aches to tell about seeing a Pepsi-Cola truck, its sign reading "Come Alive!," drive into a cemetery. Three of you got lost coming to the studio. Take it from me, lady, you women in the studio audience are wonderful. With you there, I've got a good show. Without you? Lady, I'm in trouble!

Bonnie was curious one day because I called on a lady who told a hilarious story about Pampers.

"Paul," Bonnie said after the show, "how did you know she was going to come out with that?"

The warmup—that's how. Even when you women in the bleachers don't say much, I can sense which one of you is dying to blurt out something. It's not that I'm a mind-reader. It's just that I've had the pleasure of working with so many of you—day after day, year after year—that something inside me says that this woman is going to come out with a show-stopper on the air. Years of experience help me. That's the one thing they can't teach in broadcasting schools. No, you have to stand there, year after year, and grow with your audiences.

Experience guides me on the mornings when you in the audience are not as responsive as other audiences have been. I don't mean this wrongly—and when I kid about how dead the audience is, I hope you know that I'm only kidding. What I mean is, each group of women is different. Some audiences start laughing—and just won't quit. Other audiences won't start; they sit there, smile sociably, but that's all, brother! Now to be honest, both types of audiences are fine. Both of you—the laughers or the quiet-as-mouse audiences—enjoy the show because it shows in your eyes. It's just that you react differently. Well, when I get a bleacherful of quiet ones, I sense it—fast—during the warmup. So as I'm doing the warmup, I am mentally putting that day's show together.

"We'll play more music," I'll tell myself. "And we'll read more letters."

Other days, when you women just won't quit laughing, I can sense that before the show starts, too; so I tell myself: "Well, first I'll call on that lady. Then I'll go to that one. And that one. And that one. . . ."

And on and on and on.

So that is why I like to do the warmup personally. And, to be fair, even though I do the warmups, I still don't know what will happen. If I did, there are mornings I would have stayed in bed! When the Dixon Show doesn't get rolling, the fault doesn't lie with anyone but me. And I know it.

So if I'm wrong for letting the audience see me before the show, so be it. I'll keep on being wrong that way even though it ain't good "show business." I know it isn't good show business, you know it, and so does everyone, but that kind of show business is foreign to me. I toss the old show business rules out the window and make up my own as I go along. Maybe that's why our show is different.

So much for show business. And so much for the guy in Cologne, Germany, who said: "Zxcvbnmlkjhgf-dsaqwertyuiop!!!"

Well, promptly at 8:58—two minutes before we go on the network—I introduce Bruce and his band to the audience. Then I introduce whichever of the three girls will be with me that day. Then we fool around till 9:00, the red tally lights come on—and brother, that's it. I take the gum from my mouth, toss it over my shoulder so it lands behind the set—there must be a million pieces of my gum back there!—and we're on the air.

The warmup has helped me. I don't know whether it helped the studio audience, because the last thing

I say is: "Girls, you might as well enjoy the show. You can't get out—because the doors are locked."

I say this every day, but the day I remember best was the time when—during the show—a grandmother who was sweet as can be walked up to Bruce and whispered in his ear. They were both off camera at the time, so I handed the microphone to Bonnie, and went over to see—off camera, of course—what was going on. The grandmother looked flustered and whispered to me: "Paul Baby, somebody better open those doors quick!"

And off she trotted.

Mercy! What's a grandmother to do!

Well, that's how—in one fashion or another—we get the show on the air. On special days, like Christmas or Thanksgiving, we'll tape the shows ahead of time and the routine will vary, but not greatly. Funny thing about those shows we do tape: I never watch them. I've yet to see myself on television. I mean that. And when we make audio tapes, recording only the sound portion, I never listen to an entire show—only a commercial on rare occasions. Why don't I watch myself? For two reasons: one, I'll worry about how awful I am; and two, I can't stand me on the air!

No need to tell you what happens on the show each day. You've seen me work. The same thing happens today that happened yesterday. Come back in ten years and we'll be doing the same darned show. Face it. The only reason women watch is they're hooked, waiting for us to do something different!

When 10:30 rolls around and we wave goodby, no whistle toots to end the day for me. The day is just beginning. Fun and games are over for me; and I

mean it, the show is fun. My shirt is soaking wet as
I stand around to chat a little longer with the audi-
ence. I answer questions, some of which have been
included in this book, and I give out autographs where
I can, but (darn him!) Scratchy gives out more than
I do. And so does Bruce. And Colleen. And Bonnie.
And Marian. That shows where I stand!

The amenities being over, I hurry back to my office to do whatever awaits me. First, I change my
shirt, putting the wet one in my briefcase. I don't
know what other men carry in their briefcases, but
I carry dirty laundry in mine—and nothing else. I
knew men in New York who carried lunches in theirs.
One carried a bar, except for the ice. One man whom
we considered abnormal used his to lug papers.

If Bill McCluskey doesn't come around for a meeting with a client, chances are an advertising agency
man is waiting to fill me in on a new product. The
telephone rings a thousand times—from clients; production people; advertising agency men; our Chicago,
Hollywood, and New York sales offices; and a few
wrong numbers. The morning goes swiftly. I hardly
have time to change shirts before lunch, but I make
time for that. Who wants to run around soaked? On
those rare mornings when there is no meeting, I
wander down into the basement of Radio Studio E
where Bruce's group is rehearsing with one of the
girls. We'll sit around, making smalltalk, pretending
to work. Those mornings are rare. But they are relaxing.

Lunch? It's a continuation of business, lady. If I'm
not having lunch with this client, I'm having lunch
with that one. I don't eat much lunch. My diet, you

know. Perhaps I'll have a salad or a sandwich. Or, now and then, I'll have a small steak. I'm usually too busy enjoying the company because the business-men I come in contact with are friends as well as business associates. They're a great bunch. Proof of that was the thing Avco put on with Bob Hope to raise money for his local Hope House. The businessmen made that promotion a success. Without them, we'd have been lost.

That promotion started when Bob Hope and John Murphy shared a speaker's table at some banquet. Bob Hope spotted John Murphy's name tag, saw he was from Cincinnati, and before you could blink, Hope and Murphy were thick as two peas in a pod, figuring out ways to raise money for the Hope House here.

Do you remember the Bob Hope Benefit Golf Match when Bob Hope, Arnold Palmer, and Perry Como came to Cincinnati to help Judge Benjamin Schwartz with Hope House? That place where the teenage boys lived needed a new fire-escape, a new roof, work on the heating system—lots of stuff. The building is over 130 years old. Well, thanks to John Murphy and Bob Hope, Avco helped out with a crackerjack of a pro-motion. Didn't make a dime on the deal, either. That's a side of Murphy and Avco the public doesn't hear about.

How did Bob Hope feel about John Murphy's ef-forts? Well, he wrote to John that "when you start to do something, John, you do it the right way." Murphy tries to pass the credit along to the rest of us, but fair's fair. He and Hope, via long-distance calls that worried John's wife Win (first she thought a drunk was calling instead of Hope!) because these calls came out of her budget, worked out the details by which Cincinnati businessmen would pay $500 each to play a few rounds with the famous trio. In addition, other men paid $100 just to caddy! I came into the picture because I called the businessmen I knew and asked them to fork over the $500—to play themselves or to sponsor players. To show what great guys these Midwest businessmen are, I had to spend only a few hours on the telephone before the event was sold out!

Can you see, lady, why I have a warm spot in my heart for these men? Even now I can recite—from memory of that afternoon on the telephone—those who said yes. Let's see, those who paid the $500 for three rounds with Hope, Palmer and Como were: Ron Ullett who was sponsored by the *Cincinnati Enquirer;* Frank Van Lahr who was then president of the Provident Bank; Waite Hoyt was there sponsored by (of course) Burger Beer; the Hudepohl Brewing Company sponsored Ed Kennedy; WCPO-TV sponsored Al Schottelkotte; J. W. Lear, the president of the Welfare Finance Corporation, was there; J. Barrett Buse, husband of Annie and also connected with the Buse Distillers was in on the action; and—

That reminds me. You wouldn't call Barry Buse one of the lower wage earners, but what I wanted to tell you was about the time Annie had her baby and we announced it over the Dixon Show because—well, as you know I'm a blabbermouth. Not too many people knew who Barry Buse was. Bonnie would say: "Who had a baby?"

"Annie Buse," I would say.

Bonnie would be more confused than ever.

"Who is Annie Buse?" she would ask politely.

"Barry Buse's wife," I would explain.

That confused Bonnie completely.

"But *who* is Barry Buse?" she said.

"Annie's husband," I said.

Clear as mud? Bonnie is still confused. But we did send the new mother a WLW-Television Care Package filled with odds and ends from the studios: Pampers, Gerber Baby Food, stuff like that. And a pair of scissors—so the kid could clip coupons like its old man.

So much for my good friends the Barry Buses. The point is, when you have a friend like Dixon, you don't need enemies—or anything else for that matter. But they're grand people, both of them: Barry Buse and his wife Annie; as well as Annie and her husband Barry Buse. All four of them are swell. But where was I? Oh yes, listing participants in the golf thing.

Well, other $500 participants were Common Pleas Judge Ralph B. Kohnen; Walter E. Beckjord, Jr., the vice president and general counselor for the Cincinnati Gas and Electric Company; Frank Mayfield, Jr.; and WKRC's Tom Jones was there, sponsored by Mrs. A. B. Cohen, better known and more affectionately known simply as Dolly. Hello, Dolly! And there was one other. *I* played, too.

Did I pay $500? No, because Bonnie Lou wouldn't lend me the money. But Avco sponsored me. And they sponsored me in addition to all the other bucks they tossed—free—into the till to make sure the event was a success.

The honorary caddies who paid $100? Well, Pepsi-Cola sponsored Walter Gross: WKRC-TV sponsored Burch Riber; Knodel Tygrett sponsored Harry Knodel,

Jim Tygrett, and Dick Schieman; Manufacturers'
representative Bill Makepeace was there; so was Hank
Purcell who used to be with Procter and Gamble; don't
forget Joe Brant, the lawyer; and there was Art Radt-
ke sponsored by the Cincinnati Air Conditioning Company; Woody Sander Ford sponsored Charles Ram-
pello; John Rosenthal was sponsored by all the other
Rosenthals—and there are thousands of them—at
S. Rosenthal Printers; and naturally Don Mergard
was there, sponsored by the Mergard Bowling and
Trophy Company.

Most of these, as I say, are businessmen who are
also my friends. So when I have a business lunch I
don't mind. Anyway, that takes care of my lunch,
but my day is still not over. I go back to the office
to tackle paperwork—mounds of it! Unless, of course,
two or three *more* meetings have been scheduled!!!

Can you see why I don't make as many personal
appearances as I used to make? Not complaining, but
this show has grown. We have details to take care of
now that we never dreamed about when we first went
on the air. 'Course, in those days we didn't have many
sponsors, either. Now—as of this minute—we have
fourteen sponsors waiting in the wings for a chance
to advertise their products. I guess there are many
ways to measure success—money isn't the only way—
but where commercial television is concerned money
is one way, isn't it?

The fact sponsors are waiting in line means that
they are waiting for you—not for me, lady. They want
to use our show to tell you what they're selling. It is
your acceptance of us that has the sponsors waiting.
We can't take the credit for it. If you women weren't

there, we'd have no sponsors. That's why this isn't bragging. How can I brag about something that you have made happen? I mean this—sincerely.

Because our bunch—the ones on camera and all the unseen others who help us put the show together—respect you, we go out of our way to see that you're treated right. A good example of this is the mail we get. Thousands of letters—and I'm not fibbing. But just about every letter we receive gets an answer—and not some quickie printed form reply. Oh, I'll be honest and say that when you write in for tickets and that's all your letter is about, you'll get a postcard telling you you're on the waiting list. But every letter is answered. And ticket requests are answered personally when you write about other than just the tickets. We feel if you take the time to write, we should have the good manners to reply.

Somehow or other 5:30 comes. By then, lady, I'm pooped. I've been going since 7:45 or 8:00 that morning with no time off for good behavior. So you see doing the show is only a small part of getting the show on the air. Why, there are times we have been so busy that I hardly have time to run upstairs during the Vivienne Della Chiesa Show and run the camera!

When 5:30—or later—does come, I'm off to the parking lot, and driving back along Columbia Parkway. *I'm going home.* I think that's the nicest part of any husband and father's day, don't you? When he starts that trip to the sanctuary of his own front door —and to the love of his family there.

My evenings? I'm not a performer then; I'm just another guy in the neighborhood. Before dinner I'll sit around, reading the paper and relaxing with a Diet

Pepsi. I'll hear Marge in the kitchen, rattling dishes and creating dinner. Pam and Greg will probably be in their rooms, doing homework. Pam goes to the University of Cincinnati, but she's still my little girl. Greg goes to Xavier High. He's my pal—I love that gangling guy! And Pepper, the Dalmatian who is Greg's dog, will be moseying around the house, waiting for me to take him for his—and my—evening stroll. Dinner will be a family gathering, each of us trying to tell the rest about what happened during the day. Greg and I always lose that battle; who can outtalk Marge and Pam!

What do we usually eat for dinner? Steaks—if I can convince Marge they're good seven dinners a week. When we cook outside in the summer the steaks are my department, but when the weather is chilly, I sometimes trust Marge with the meat. We don't have steak *every* day; Marge is firm about that. But I keep telling her we must consider my diet. And as I tell others when we are in some fancy restaurant, I'd rather not order complicated gourmet foods.

"I'm a meat and potato man," I'll say. "And I'll have a salad instead of the potatoes, please."

The plain truth is, I don't go for dishes that are too fancy. What's wrong with a good steak?

After dinner—and after the dishes are done—I'll get Pepper and we'll go for an evening stroll. Happens every night unless the weather is too bad. We walk a mile and a half. He gets a kick out of our evening stroll and so do I. Sometimes Greg will come along. I like those evenings best. There's something satisfying in taking a stroll with a son who can match his old man, stride for stride. I wouldn't trade those evenings for all the tea in China.

On nights when just Pepper and I get our exercise,
I daydream as we walk along. We pass house after
house that has lights on. Inside, through the picture
windows, I can see the blue glare that means the television is on. Powerful thing—this television. Scary,
too. Colleen said she couldn't conceive of all the people who watch us each morning. "Put them into one
auditorium," she murmured, "and I'd die of fright. I
could never face them. . . ." But the secret is, we don't
perform before an auditorium filled with people. Oh,
we do when our show goes to other cities, but you
know what I mean. We perform for one living room at
a time—times how many thousand! That's why I'm
intrigued as I pass the houses that have the televisions
on. Was I in that living room that morning? And
that one, and that one, and that one? You feel awfully small thinking of that. What right have you to
visit those homes? What entertainment can you hope
to offer?

It is during moments of thinking this that I wish
I did have some talent—other than just talking. I
would like to do something nice for these people who
have me in their homes each day.

And so I walk on, fast, wondering when the viewers will wake up to the fact that I get more from
them than I ever give back. Pepper wags his tail—
and I turn my steps to home. I'm an awfully lucky
man when you think about it. Each day I have a different cast of 150 women! Kneesville! That ever-
changing little community of the most beautiful
women in the world! So I really don't do the same
show every day. How could I? Each day we have 150
brand new participants! Who else gets all the help

I get? When you have no talent, lady, you need all the help—and loving—you can lay your hands on.

By the time I reach home again, the house has settled down, running at half speed. Marge and I talk some more—and some more. Or, watch television together. By eleven, the lights are off—unless one of the kids is cramming for a test. We don't stay up all hours because we can't. I have to be up again at six. Even when we go visiting on week nights, we come home early. Sure, it would be fun to stay out, but I would rather be fresh in the morning than enjoy one extra hour in the evening. Marge understands. So do our friends.

On Saturdays during the winter I do odd jobs the same as any father. Next Saturday, for instance, I have to get a filter for the furnace. On Sunday, there's church—and just plain relaxing afterward. In the summer? Lady, in the summer my weekends are one grand, glorious, wonderful visit to the golf course. Greg has started to play golf, too. He's beginning to beat me. Is that any way for a boy to treat his dad?

So that's a typical weekday for me. Some work, some fun, and an evening stroll with Pepper. But, as I said earlier, our show is more than me. Let me tell of the others, too. And, most important, I must tell you how our show started on WLW-Television. It was not my dream. It was the dream of another guy. But thanks to his dream, my dreams have come true.

Who is that fellow? Well, lady, his name is John Murphy. So put your hand over your heart—and read on!

# 10.

## Paul Baby &

# JOHN MURPHY

☆ "I'm confused," one of you girls said. "Sometimes you make John Murphy sound nice as pie. But sometimes you make him sound terrifying. Which is the *real* John Murphy?"

That question isn't easy to answer because it is hard to get the real John Murphy to stand up, sit down, wave, or do anything. There are a whole bunch of John Murphys—and all of them are important to me.

Just as Mort Watters came along at one right moment to point me in the right direction, John Murphy came along at another. You might say everything that I am today I owe to Mort Watters, John Murphy, and Shillito's. What I owe to Shillito's is easiest to list.

The store thoughtfully sends me itemized bills each month, listing the amount. Marge is responsible for that. She wears out a charge plate a month.

But this book is not about Marge's collection of charge plates. This is about behind the scenes of television. Since this book *is* about behind the scenes, John Murphy must be included because if it weren't for him, half the behinds would not be in television today. That doesn't sound right, but you know what I mean. When many of us think of John Murphy, we put out hands over our hearts and sing: "You made me what I am today. . . ."

So which is the real John Murphy? Frankly, lady, I don't know. Let's take a good look at him and maybe we can find out together.

Well, the first time I met John Murphy was at a party WCPO-TV threw. Mort Watters had invited the leaders of the city so naturally John was among those present. Our first meeting was dramatic.

John looked at me and said: "Oh, hello."

I looked at him and said: "Oh, hello."

Someone else came up, started a conversation with John, they wandered off together, and there I stood, drinking my Diet Pepsi. Later, whenever John and I met, we would carry on the brilliant conversation we had started at our first meeting. And we met lots of places: on the street, on the street, on the street, and —once—on Garfield Place. Each time, John would say: "Oh, hello."

But sometimes John would be in a hurry. He'd not have the time then to get "Oh, hello," all the way out. Those times he would say "Oh, hello," but he would leave off the "o." You can tell that I impressed him.

Sometimes, actually, he would be too awed to speak.
When he saw me coming he would cross quickly to the
other side of the street. Or he would duck down an
alley. Or hide in a doorway.

Charlton Wallace who was writing then about television in the *Cincinnati Times-Star* also went out
of his way to see that John and I got to know one
another better. Charlton, the same as Mary Wood,
was responsible via the television columns for bringing many of us to the attention of the public in
those early days. So this chapter hasn't even got rolling and already I'm wrong. I owe as much to friends
like Charlton and Mary as I do to Mort Watters, John
Murphy, and Shillito's.

Anyway, as the result of meeting John Murphy so
much and saying hello to him a lot, I got to know him
better. In fact, before I left Cincinnati for New York,
John and I were on familiar terms. We no longer said
"Hello" when we met. I would say "Hi." John would
simply nod his head but sometimes—for the sake
of variety—he would start shaking it. Actually, none
of this *explains* which is the real John Murphy, does
it? So let me try another way.

As I said before, there are many John Murphys. One
is *JOHN MURPHY THE TYPICAL NEW YORKER.*
No question about him being that because once he
told me: "I'm from the Bronx, but I married Win
who was from Brooklyn. Before our marriage, I lived
in Manhattan. After our marriage, we lived in Queens.
We've lived in four of the five boroughs. The only one
we missed was Staten Island." He thought a minute,
then added, "If the bridge had been in existence at
the time, we would have probably lived *there,* too!"

In other words, John Murphy isn't the product of a 4-H Club. His mother didn't even have a windowbox. But let's take a look at another John Murphy: *JOHN MURPHY THE YOUNG MAN WHO WAS START-ING OUT TO MAKE HIS WAY IN THE WORLD.* He didn't start out as president of Avco Broadcasting. He began as an NBC pageboy in New York in 1930. He wasn't a rich kid. He had to struggle the way the rest of us did. While he was still in his teens, his father died; and a month after he went to work for NBC, his mother died. So he was on his own. He divided his time between being an NBC pageboy, a drummer in a small combo, and—as he says—"getting some schooling in."

"John Murphy is a musician?" you ask.

Yes, lady, and a darned good one. But he no longer plays club dates, if that helps. He still has his drums, but he says of them: "They are getting less and less exposure."

Even in those early days John was impressed with radio. He can recall sitting with his mother, listening to the 1924 convention on their crystal set. Mostly, though, John listened in because in that era great bands like Hal Kemp and Guy Lombardo played their hearts out on the radio. But John points out, that was *before* the Dorsey Brothers had got off the ground, though the Wright Brothers—Orville and Wilbur— had.

While a pageboy at NBC John Murphy met—distantly, of course—George Washington Hill of the American Tobacco Company and the Lucky Strike Hit Parade.

"Hill would stride into the NBC conference room

every Saturday morning," John said, "and sit there, listening to the music. And he would have to get up while the music played and dance to it. That was the only way he could be sure of the tempo. The reason I know is that I set up the conference room for the meeting: put out ashtrays, writing pads, water glasses, and the rest. Everything you ever heard about George Washington Hill was true. But he was a terrific person and a successful businessman so he must have been doing *something* right."

The *JOHN MURPHY THE NBC PAGEBOY* was lucky—and admits it. He always managed to work at NBC as a page on Saturday afternoon when the network broadcast football games. He wasn't *that* interested in football; he was more interested in the stand-by musicians who were there to play music in case the line to the football game broke.

John and the musicians would listen to the game— "Depending on who was playing," John said, "and only if the interest was keen"—and when not doing that, they would have jam sessions. Benny Goodman played saxophone as a house musician, the Dorsey Brothers were sitting in, and so was Phil Napoleon. Who played drums? The NBC pageboy named John Murphy!

What about *JOHN MURPHY THE DRUMMER IN HIS OWN LITTLE COMBO*? That is *another* John Murphy. His group started out as five fellows who played the Sunday night dance at the Holy Name Church in Manhattan. Soon the group increased to ten because, as John said, "Success breeds ambition— and ambition breeds success." Finally they found themselves either going to school or working during the day and playing four nights a week.

Now if you'll point the camera over to this side of the studio, Gordy, we'll show the girls another John Murphy: *JOHN MURPHY OF THE NBC STENO-GRAPHIC DEPARTMENT*. He transferred from NBC page to that because the band was almost too success-ful—and he wasn't getting much sleep. As a member of the stenographic department he had Sundays off —and since the band usually played till 2:00 A.M. Sunday morning—well, there you are!

Even after the transfer he still wandered around pooped. So he had to make a decision: go with the band full time or go into broadcasting full time. What forced the decision was the chance his band had to play six nights a week, as opposed to one-night stands, at the Hunter Island Inn, a saxophone toot up the road from the Glenn Island Casino where Glenn Gray and the Dorsey Brothers had got their first big break.

"Was the decision hard to make?" I asked him.

He nodded.

"The important thing," he said, "was did I want to grow with broadcasting or be a musician. Actually, I was making more money with my drums than I was at NBC, but my guardian angel was working overtime. Anyway, I knew in my heart I wasn't a *good* musician. I was a good drummer, I suppose, because they said I had a beat. But I didn't really understand music. I was faking most of the time. So I took a hard look at broadcasting, where it was going, and how it was developing. About this time I had moved into the traffic department and into the business side of broadcasting. The traffic department was where the stations along the network cleared for commercial programming. This was back in the mid-thirties. But the decision? Now that I look back on it, I have to admit I was getting guidance from Someone. . . ."

I for one am glad John chose broadcasting. Without him, I'd be a nothing today—and that's God's truth. That is why John deserves a big place in this book. If he'd stayed with the drums I'd have had no reason to write a book at all. There's another reason I'm glad he gave up the drums for broadcasting. Suppose things had happened the other way: Marvin Cox might have ended up our fearless leader!

Mercy!

It was back then in those thirties that another John Murphy emerged: *THE JOHN MURPHY WHO WAS GETTING HIS FEET WET IN BROADCASTING AS A MEMBER OF THE NBC TRAFFIC DEPARTMENT.* In that department John was exposed to just about every kind of radio operator on the air. He would visit the NBC affiliates, work with them, adjust their complaints, and carry their thoughts back to the higher echelon in New York.

"WLW was one of the stations I called on," he remembers. His last position at NBC was as division manager of Station Relations. Television was coming along, but the infant industry still wore electronic Pampers. Television was the reason John left NBC and came here. He had been interested in the new industry a long time, his interest coming to life even before World War II. In those early days NBC sent crews to Yankee Stadium to televise ball games for the people who had no sets to watch. That doesn't sound right, but you know what I mean. Since John's office was down the hall from the chief engineer's, John would sneak out of the traffic department and watch the game for awhile. *He* says he strolled, but I say he sneaked. It sounds good to say that he was learning the business, but I think he was goofing off a little.

"Can you talk that way about your boss and get away with it?" I hear some of you asking.

Of course I can. But remind me to take the above paragraph out of the book before it gets published, will you? After all, there's a John Murphy I'd rather not meet: that's the *JOHN MURPHY WHO CAN FIRE ME.* If I forget to take the paragraph out of the book, do me a favor. Pretend you never read it.

Now, where was I? Oh yes, saying nice things about Mr. Murphy. Yoo-hoo, Mr. Murphy! Hi there! How's the family?

Now, Gordy, if you will point the camera over there we'll introduce still another John Murphy: *THE JOHN MURPHY WHO LEFT NEW YORK TO COME TO OHIO AND DO NICE THINGS TO TELEVISION AROUND HERE.* Why did he leave New York and come to Ohio? Well, as an NBC official he had traveled the Midwest, but he wanted to get into television at the station level—and he wanted just the right station. When Bob Dunville asked him to put WLW-D on the air in Dayton in 1949, John jumped at the chance. He didn't last long there, though; that's what he told me.

"Why?" I said. "Were you fired?"

He gave me a look.

"Sorry I asked," I said quickly, and went about my

business which was, at the time, shining his shoes.

John Murphy was *not* fired from WLW-D. After he had been there ten months he was asked to come down to Cincinnati and take over programming at WLW-T. Why was he asked to come to Cincinnati? I'm sorry you asked because when things are not going right he puts the blame on me.

The way he tells it: "Dixon was the big competition over at WCPO-TV, clobbering everyone. WLW-T wanted me to do something about that."

I'm glad they brought in John Murphy. Just think: they could have brought in a fast gun from the West, a hired killer, like they're always doing on television westerns.

The point is, John Murphy came to Cincinnati television—and television here hasn't been the same since. Ruth Lyons was glad to see him arrive. Before he came to handle the programming chores, Ruth was exhausting herself handling not one—but two— full-time jobs: running her show and acting as program director. Only a genius could do two jobs like that but Ruth is a genius. Some people look upon her simply as a wonderful talent and a wonderful lady. She is those things—and something else: a darned good businessman. But even so, two jobs were too much. And enter John Murphy.

John was no Johnny-come-lately at working with programs and discovering talent. Before he came to Cincinnati he had made several top discoveries. Who discovered Bob Smith—"Howdy Doody"—and brought him from Buffalo to New York and the big time? John Murphy, that's who. Who discovered Neal Val Ells in Terre Haute, Indiana, and brought him to

WLW-D to become one of the first big television announcers in the area? John Murphy, that's who. And who discovered electricity? Benjamin Franklin. I just threw that in to keep you on your toes. I saw several of you sleeping.

Now let us get a close up of another John Murphy: *PROGRAMMING GENIUS WHO SAYS HE ISN'T.* This was the John Murphy who brought Mel Martin over from WCPO, put him on a morning show, and thus put into practice one of John's pet theories which is filled with not-so-common sense. As John says: "You don't have to be a mental genius to understand that if you have an audience of adults you sell products better than if the audience is only children. That's why I wanted a live *adult* show in the morning. Children might have some influence, but if you can have adults watching, your sponsors will be happy. And your shows will be a success."

And John knows whereof he speaks. Proof of that is, after putting together the Mel Martin Show, he auditioned it for Albers and sold the show even *before* it went on the air. That brings us to another John Murphy: *JOHN MURPHY THE SUPER SALESMAN.* To be a programming genius is one thing, but he's doubly blessed. He can peddle what he believes in. Thank goodness he believes in the Brauns, Della Chiesas, and Dixons! But even a super salesman has his off days. John is the first to admit it.

Take the business of Mel Martin. As some of you may recall, Mel—one of the real nice guys in the business—left television for the ministry—at the height of his television success, too. Some people thought his interest in the ministry was phony, but

John Murphy will tell anyone how wrong that is.
John told me: "I know that Mel was serious because when he said he wanted to leave, I offered
him a religious program on WLW-T. He was polite,
but he said to do a television show was completely
contrary to his feelings. That's how he put it. I respected him for that. I stopped trying to sell him the
idea of a religious show. And I still respect him. Good
people like him are wonderful to know—if only for a
little while. . . ."

So that was when the master salesman struck out—
but do you blame him? I don't.

So there was John Murphy wanting to put on a
live show in the morning for adults—and having no
suitable talent to do it with. Then we left WCPO-TV
and went into New York when Dumont asked me
to originate our network show from there. But WCPO-
TV couldn't carry us in Cincinnati, so John got us on
WLW-T. He told me later that the moment he was
aware that our New York show would be carried over
WLW-T in an afternoon time period, he and Harry
LeBrun—super salesmen both!—got into action. The
two of them went to the Cuvier Press Club for lunch,
got on a telephone and stayed on it till three that
afternoon. When they hung up, they had sold every
spot availability our show had!

Avco just naturally seems to attract the real professionals of the business. Consider Walter Bartlett, now
the vice president in charge of sales. And guys like
Mike Kievman and Clyde Haenle and Jack Heywood!
These behind-the-scenes good guys save many a television and a corporate day! Consider the men Avco
has at its sister stations, real professionals at sales

and management. There's Don Meineke, Charlie Mc-
Fadden, and Ray Poland in Dayton; Lloyd Forrest and
Dick Reed in Columbus; and in Indianapolis there's
Pat Shannon and Jerry Blankenbeker.

But of all the good guys in the white hats at Avco,
I'd personally be lost without John Murphy—and I'm
not taking any credit away from any of the others
when I say this. John himself tries to dodge praise by
saying I'm easy to sell.

"You really know how to sell products," he keeps
saying.

Well, I've got news for you, Mr. Murphy. I couldn't
sell a thing—if you didn't get the clients with the
products to sell. So there! Stop being so modest.

Shortly after selling clients on the idea of me, John
Murphy came to New York and visited our television
studios. Afterward, he had dinner with Marge and
me. We talked about many things—television and
raising kids. Our Pam and John Murphy's daughter
Pat had been friends before we had left for New
York. When fathers have beautiful daughters, the
conversation just naturally ain't all business! But after
John left that evening, talk about being homesick!
Marge and I loved New York, we don't put it down,
but I guess we are just not the New York types. Certainly Pam and Greg aren't. Those two kids could
never believe in our own home in the New York suburbs. They still thought our real home was back in
Cincinnati—and that New York was only temporary.
John Murphy's visit had brought everything into
focus: New York was great, but the Dixons didn't
want to live there.

And here again, I must be honest and thank John

Murphy because he personally made it possible for
Marge, Pam, Greg, and me to say good-by to New
York and to say hello (again!) with love to the Mid-
west.

So that's *another* John Murphy: *JOHN MURPHY
THE FRIEND.*

When I came back I did the same kind of show
I had always done: record pantomime. The show was
seen in Cincinnati, Dayton, and Columbus. I suppose
the show was good enough. But something had happened to television, hadn't it? When television was
new, a pantomime record show could capture the
imaginations of viewers. But television had matured
and our show hadn't. It was just creaking along, no
longer setting the world on fire, just doing pretty
good—and no more. When John Murphy called me
to his office I was scared. I thought I was going to be
given the sack. But I reckoned without John.

I can still remember sitting in his office and feeling
relief flood me as he explained his programming
dream: a *live* morning show aimed at an *adult* audience. He had tinkered with the dream with Mel Martin. Now he was dusting off that dream and asking
me if I wanted to make it a reality.

"With a studio audience, Paul," he said. "And with
a band. No records. What do you think?"

I wasn't sure. My broadcast career till then had
been with recorded music.

"Do *you* think I can do it?" I said finally.

He nodded.

And that was that!

There he was going out on a limb for me the same
as he goes out on the limb every hour of every work-

ing day for his staff. But this is the John Murphy
you never hear about. To be honest, this is the John
Murphy that he himself tries to keep hidden because
he feels it is not important. He loves live programs
and live talent—and more important, he loves for
them to be local. And, as the result, there he usually
sits out on a limb and enjoying every minute of it.

"Besides," he said, trying to change the subject but
in this book he can't, "it's good business to use local
talent on WLW-Television. We can promote the
Dixons, Brauns, and Della Chiesas—and the rest. This
gives us a sales advantage and a programming advantage over our competition. How can you promote a
movie or a syndicated show? With our people we can
build promotions around them. It's a matter of finding
the right talent. That's all. We've had our share of
flops. Don't forget that. But our flops are few and far
between. . . ."

Once in a rare and mellow mood John Murphy said
to me: "Sure, Paul, I go out on limbs all the time.
Once you get into management, you have to—or
you're doing nothing to earn your keep. And whatever
you do, you have to be successful at it or you're in
trouble. These are the facts I live with every day.
The thing is, you can't be successful by standing still
or doing nothing."

He was silent for a moment, then added: "I don't
know which of us has the most fun, Paul. All I know
is, when you're out there in front of that camera, you
must make minute-by-minute and second-by-second
decisions that concern today. I sit here and make decisions that will affect Avco five, ten, fifteen years from
now. It's fun, Paul, and it's rewarding, too. And it's

no more frightening than watching someone putting one of those $20,000 putts we see on televised tournaments. One difference is, the golfer sees the result right away. And there's another difference. Some of my decisions can cost the company a lot more than $20,000."

So, lady, there you are. As you can see, there are so many John Murphys running around that we can get bewildered, can't we? There's John Murphy the NBC page. There's John Murphy the drummer. And John Murphy *this!* And John Murphy *that!*

For goodness sake, will the *real* John Murphy please sit down!

# 11.
# Paul Baby &
# THE BAND

☆ More questions from the studio audience:

"Don't you realize what a great musician Bruce Brownfield is?" a woman once scolded me after the show. "Why are you always telling him to shut up?"

"But, lady," I said, "Bruce knows I'm kidding."

"Are you sure?" she said, looking at me carefully. "He seems so sweet."

"Sure I'm sure," I said. "I—"

"Just because *you* can't play the accordion!" she sniffed, went over to get Bruce's autograph, and left me with my bare face hanging out. There was no way to convince her, but maybe I can convince you. Simply put, Bruce Brownfield and his band are great—and they know that I know it.

Look at it this way. To find five musicians who do other things besides play music ain't easy. I mean, in an ordinary band, a drummer plays drums. Period. The same thing applies to other musicians. They play their instruments and between numbers they sit there, read a racing form, and that is that. But on the Dixon Show every man in that band is a ham— and a performer in his own right.

Take roll call and see for yourself. Marvin Cox, the drummer, is a funny, *funny* guy; and you girls in the audience know it. Jerry Haggerty who plays saxophone is one of the finest *singers* you'd ever want to meet. Also, he comes up with some real wild lines on the show. Larry Downing who plays the bass is a classic with that high-voice version of the Ink Spots. I keep telling him to shut up, but if he does I'm dead. Mel Horner on guitar is a comedian who comes up with the craziest lines. These fellows feed me so many lines during the course of a show that it's unbelievable, but I don't use all of them on the air. If I did, we wouldn't be on the air!

As for Bruce, he is as much a part of our show as I am and the girls are. Actually, we're a team and a family. You won't catch me going on personal appearances without them. I need them. Without them, I'm nothing—and I'll be the first to admit it.

One thing bothers me, though. When we do personal appearances together, Bruce gives out more autographs than *I* do! Don't give me that look, lady. I'm only kidding! As far as I'm concerned, Bruce is one of the nicest guys in the business. He goes around, not hurting anyone. Well, at least he tries to be that way, but now and then, things don't work out like that. He once hurt the feelings of a cello player's wife.

Not *intentionally*, but that's the way wives of cello players are. Bruce tells it this way:

"This cello player had come on the Dixon Show as a guest, but he appeared too late to rehearse. No strain. Only he passed out arrangements written in the European style with the chord symbols different than we were used to. I told him we couldn't play those arrangements because we couldn't read them and we'd only make hash of his playing. Right on the air, his wife got angry. Brrr!"

Bruce sighed, adding: "I suppose we could have faked it, but I was afraid we'd murder the background."

That's the kind of a guy Bruce is. He's kind but he's also a professional. Bruce has another side, too.

"How did we get Marvin Cox?" he said. "Well, we got him from Clyde McCoy. We traded two old tuba players and picked Marvin up on waivers."

Marvin, who has been with our show nearly three years, is one of the world's greatest drummers. No one can carry that man's sticks. He's one of the world's greatest comedians, too. Each day the engineers put his microphone in a different—and harder to reach— place. Sometimes they put it under the drums. Sometimes they hide it on the wall. Once, during the Christmas season, they hid it in a Christmas wreath. Marvin manages to find it and talk into it. He gets in some weird positions, though, doing that. But trust him, whatever the position, to come through with lines that are humdingers.

And he also came up with a thousand pairs of booties when his wife had her baby. To show how close you ladies are to our gang, I think that every one of you suffered right along with Marvin (and *us*) waiting for his baby to be born. And afterward? Well, you flooded the little kid with gifts that wouldn't quit.

When Bruce and the band played at the opening of the Provident Bank they hardly had time to play. Most of you people who filed by kept asking Marv how the baby was.

"He's either got to stop having babies," Bruce shrugged, "or stop going on remotes with us."

Do the guys in the band liven up our show? You bet! Bruce has given me more program material than I can use in a lifetime—and he gives it without even trying. I guess you might say we enjoy being together. On some shows, the band stays still, just sitting there. On our show, those nuts are always doing something! And they're always having babies. At least, their wives are.

When Bruce's wife Mildred had their last child Steven, she sure helped peddle a lot of Partridge wieners. We had the running gag—which you all know by heart, of course—that Mildred would wake up in the middle of the night, craving a Partridge wiener. *Not* boiled. *Not* fried. Not *cold*. But *grilled* on an outdoor grill!

And—so the gag would go—out would go Bruce in the wee hours into his backyard, set up the grill, start the fire, and grill her what she wanted. And he would say: "The neighbors who saw me around the fire grilling one wiener were about to have me taken away."

How long did that gag go on? Till Mildred had the

baby. And for a long time afterward. The gags on our show stick around, don't they? That's why you know what I'm going to say before I open my mouth. If we ever used new material, mercy! It wouldn't be our show.

As for being a professional, Bruce is more the professional than I am. He has been with Avco Broadcasting since 1950. A native of Covington, Kentucky, he attended the College of Music and the Cincinnati Conservatory. During World War II he was in the navy. His pastimes, he insists, are household repairs and family duties "like any other guy." So you can see he's no great prima donna. Bruce and Mildred now live in Fort Wright, Kentucky, with their two sons, Bruce and Steve, and their daughter Dinah.

He comes from a musical family, too. His father was one of the first musicians to be hired at WLW. That's back in the 1930's. Later, his father and Ruth Lyons used to work together at WKRC. When Bruce would play on the 50-50 Club during the Ruth Lyons regime, she would always kid him because when she first met Bruce, he was a toddler.

Who hired Bruce at WLW-Television? John Murphy! In fact, Bruce was the first person Mr. Murphy hired when he came to WLW. Bruce had just come back from Florida where, with his trio, he had got a suntan and nightclub experience. Prior to Florida, Bruce and the trio had been on the Arthur Godfrey and the Talent Scout program. The group was so good they were on that show more than three months!

When Bruce came to work at WLW-Television, he

worked with the Dick Hageman Show, the Walt Phillips Show, and a show with Ruby Wright. And —when there were no shows open for his trio—he and the boys would struggle into the station before sunup to provide music for "Chore Time," the 5 A.M. farm show.

"Can you imagine Larry at that hour?" Bruce grinned. "Gosh, he has a hard time waking up to do the Dixon Show!"

Larry Downing and Mel Horner have both been with Bruce since their first days at WLW. Whether the musicians in Bruce's band have been there a long time or are newcomers, he has collected a group that is tops. I had the hardest time convincing them that they shouldn't play music which pleased other musicians; I wanted them to play music that would satisfy you and me—and, lady, face it, neither one of us is going to play in a symphony orchestra. The point is, because I'm corny I happen to think people like the kind of music they can understand. I don't mean the old four-beat Guy Lombardo stuff, but gutsy music that is good and also understandable.

As Bruce says: "We play the standards, but if a good pop tune comes along, we'll use it. Standards seem to be the music that goes best at the hour of the morning we're on the air."

I get many letters saying that Bruce is a dreamboat and a wonderful guy. But they never ask me what Bruce is really like. Bruce is always asked, "What is that nut Dixon really like?" I guess the reason people don't ask about Bruce is that they can tell the kind of guy he is. He's one of the real dear people that God

☆ Ruby and I didn't have to do the show in Versailles, but we went anyway. And since we had nothing else to do, we went out in the woods and hunted butterflies. Here, Ruby shows Vivienne Della Chiesa and Bonnie some of our finds.

☆ When the Dracket company offered two automobiles in a promotion for Liquid Drano and Liquid Vanish, we received 170,000 pieces of mail in four weeks.

☆ Peter Grant is a darned good announcer. He can read a telephone book and give that pageful of names so much meaning that you end with a lump in your throat.

☆ See lady? I have knees too.

☆ Although Bonnie Lou and I have been together since our morning show began, she can still surprise me with new lines and mixed-up sentences which I love.

☆ Colleen Sharp *is* as little as she looks—but where everything else is concerned she's big. Big in Talent. Big in Beauty. Big in charm. Big in generosity.

☆ When Marian Spelman is working with me, another side of her comes out: the comedienne in her. I sometimes wonder what became of that shy blonde who told me she could never do the Dixon Show.

174

$396,528.92

☆ Ruth Lyons? That wonderful lady made WLW-Television what it is today!

☆ No wonder we sell Gerber Baby Food and Pampers—as well as Upjohn Unicap Seniors.

☆ On Sunday there's church—and just plain relaxing afterward with Marge, Pam, Greg, and Pepper.

ever made. In our fourteen years together, I've never been angry with him and he's never been angry with me.

The important thing is, I just couldn't work as closely with the others as I do, unless we all got along. Those of us on—and behind—the cameras have respect for one another, not just for what talents we possess, but as human beings too. Bruce feels the same way. Once, in an interview, Bruce said: "This has been a beautiful relationship, but we're positive that Paul has the best hearing of anybody in the world. Paul can hear like a cat. And he has a filter in his ear. He hears only what he wants to hear. His greatest laugh is to catch one of us daydreaming. He'll call for something right then. Anyway, we don't have too much time on his show for daydreaming. We've got too much to do and to think about. If Paul makes a funny face for the camera, Marv jumps right in with the drum. If Paul says he got a letter, presto! Off we go into our 'letter song'!"

When asked about how he started playing "On, Wisconsin" every time I mentioned that state, Bruce shrugs.

"It just happened, that's all," he says. "One day Paul said something about that cheese made up there in a little old cave in Wisconsin and . . . well, it just happened."

Bang! Now the band plays the number *all* the way through *every* time I mention the name of—no, I won't say it here. Bruce might figure out a way to play it in this book. Anyway, that song has become a trademark for our show—one of the hundred trademarks we have. Now and then I'll shout at Bruce: "You

dumb musician! Don't you know you're running a
good thing into the ground? You should stop playing
it."

When I do, some lady will shout: "Oh no, you
don't, Paul Baby! Let him play it. We like it!"

Bruce tells me that when his band plays club dates
—they play everything from barbershop openings to
the Camargo Country Club—people keep waiting for
them to break into—no, I'm still not going to say it,
but you know what I mean, don't you, lady?

As Bruce says about our show and the way I mess
it up each day: "Paul, the ladies know what's going
to happen and they *wait* for it to happen. They *want*
it to happen. You're like a firecracker about to go off.
We know the ending, but we want it anyway."

As for club dates, Bruce and his band average about
two or three engagements a week but some weeks
find them working seven nights. Bruce attributes this
to being on the show, but I say it's because his gang
is great.

"We enjoy walking along the street in Dayton,
Columbus, or Indianapolis and having people come
up and talk to us," Bruce says. He told me about New
Year's Eve when he and Marvin were returning from
a club date and they got stuck in the snow on the
interstate. "We pulled into this motel around 3 A.M.,"
he said, "and the first thing the desk clerk said was,
'Where's Paul Baby? What'd you do? Leave him out
there in the snow?'" So you see Bruce and his band
*have* to like our dumb show. No matter which way
they turn, none of you will let them forget it!

An interesting thing about Bruce and his band is
that they are five men who neither smoke nor drink.

That's a fact. I've never seen them smoke and, other than a Burger beer now and then, I've never seen them drink. However in Indianapolis last year, when we visited our salami award winner, Bruce *did* indulge. When we arrived at the house we found a buffet prepared, including a punchbowl filled with magnificent punch. That caught Bruce's eye. The poor guy was thirsty. So he headed straight to it. Go on, Bruce. You tell the rest.

"Well it was a beautiful punchbowl—" that is Bruce talking in case you've been sampling the punch yourself—"and I *was* thirsty. So I got me a cupful. It tasted so good I dipped up another. And another. And another. I didn't know the punch was laced with two fifths of sloe gin. And since I hadn't eaten since early morning, I sat there, stoned. I wasn't sure what was happening. I must have sat there twenty minutes before the world settled down again. . . ."

The world never quite settles down, though, as far as our show is concerned. Although we seem to do the same thing, day after day, Bruce and his band are ready at a moment's notice to plunge into something new musically. They do a lot of music off the cuff. They do have formal arrangements, production numbers they play, but as for the rest, anything goes. For instance, while we're reading a list of prizes, Bruce's band will go through an entire list of different songs. Listen to the show and you'll see what I mean.

Bruce is a walking encyclopedia of music. In the earlier days of our show, when sponsors were few, we'd do a thing called "Stump the Band." The standard gimmick was, some lady in the studio audience would try to request a song that Bruce didn't know. That happened seldom. But when a request did stump Bruce, the musicians were still not stumped.

"We'd play 'Stardust,' " Bruce smiled.

Bruce and I have grown up together with this morning show of ours. His band couldn't figure me out at first—and I wasn't used to "live" musicians. I had always worked with records. There is a difference between starting a record and starting live musicians. A record, poised on a spinning turntable, goes the instant the engineer releases it—and out comes music. I learned the hard way that live bands do not start that fast. Lawrence Welk has his "And uh one, and uh two." Bruce has more subtle starts but he still needs that beat, otherwise the musicians can't begin together. So I used to confuse them—and myself—when I tossed them "fast" cues. There would always be a few seconds lag between my cue and the start of the music. But Bruce was patient with me in those early days. I'm surprised that he didn't blow his top. But as you know, lady, Bruce ain't that kind of a guy. He has yet to be angry at anyone.

Now that I'm writing this chapter about Bruce and his band, I realize that some of my more enjoyable moments around the station are those moments when Bruce, the band, the girls, and I go down to the basement studio of WLW-Television and run over numbers for future Dixon Shows. Sometimes I'll sit off in a corner and listen. Other times, all of us will just sit around—and yack. In fact, the stock question his band asks is: "Well, what shall we do today—rehearse or talk?"

I've learned more about timing from Bruce and his band than they have ever learned from me since we got together. These sessions are satisfying to me and relaxing. And, as you can tell, they are not all exactly *work* sessions. Sometimes we'll sit around and talk about crab grass—or crabby children. Happily we have more of the first than of the second. Or, sometimes we'll get into deep discussions about national and international items that trouble us. Sometimes, we are so serious you'd hardly know us. But *this* side of us—the side of us that worries about crab grass and world affairs—is not the side we offer to you on the air. Who are we to be authorities on international problems? Who are we to lecture you on matters that you probably know more about than we do? So, do you mind if we keep these items back there in the privacy of that studio where, we think, they belong? Our job is to entertain you. We're not there to confuse you or make you sad.

Goodness knows, our show is sad enough as it is! And we already confuse you—and ourselves—more than enough. For instance, one morning even we were stopped in our tracks by a piano player who was the guest. The guest insisted on playing the piano— *while wearing gloves!*

Bruce is responsible for confusing an entire bank— and making the staff wonder if a robbery was in progress. He had the help of the bank president. As Bruce tells it, one morning Bruce entered the bank and the bank president sidled up and whispered in Bruce's ear so no others could hear.

"Hey," the bank president murmured like a conspirator, "can you get me some tickets to that dumb show? I'm hooked," he added, cautiously, making sure no vice presidents were listening.

Bruce got him the tickets, but told me later: "The others in the bank kept looking at us as if they suspected that the president was slipping me the combination to the vault."

One of Bruce's favorite people is Russell, the band's barber. He's not like the barber Mel tells about on the show. Mel's barber put a sign in the window of his barbershop which was being remodeled. The sign read: "During remodeling, we'll shave you in the rear."

Russell—the barber for the band—has been cutting Bruce's hair for ages. And, according to Bruce, the barber is not the greatest television fan in the world. When television first arrived in Cincinnati, Russell waited before investing in a set; he wanted to make sure that television was here to stay. I guess he had seen me and he had his doubts. When the barber finally broke down and bought a television set, the first thing he did was check the program listings. He saw that "I Love Lucy" was scheduled, and he watched the show, but the next day he was very upset.

"Listen," he told Bruce. "I thought it was going to be a *love* story!"

Then the disenchanted barber murmured into Bruce's ear: "Comb it wet or dry?"

*Comb it wet or dry?* That is what Russell asks each time, no matter how long you've been his customer. Wet or dry? Bruce must have told Russell "a million times how to comb it, but each time, he leans over and says, 'Comb it wet or dry?'"

Other than *that*, says Bruce, Russell is an excellent barber, a fine television critic, and quite sure of himself when it comes to batting averages. Well, the barber may be sure of himself, but I'm not. That's why I depend on Bruce. When one of you women in the audience stands up to ask how long I've been married, I'm not even sure of that. Before answering I'll ask Bruce: "How old is Pam?"

"Eighteen," he'll say.

"Then I've been married nineteen years, lady," I'll tell you.

Yes, I need Bruce and the others, which includes you. I've been in this business long enough to be sure of myself, but I'm still uneasy. It's as if every day the sky will fall down.

Bruce and I got to talking about this one evening. We had just finished a taping session for a holiday Dixon Show, and we were pooped. When we stopped at the Old Vienna Inn for a quick bite, our conversation drifted into that subject of my not being sure of myself.

There I was, dead tired, telling him my feelings. I was about to ramble on and on, when Bruce interrupted.

"Listen, Paul," he said, "everybody in the business wonders how he's being received. You're not alone, feeling that way. I remember when I was working the Arthur Godfrey Show. He could have done the greatest show that day, but afterward, he was always asking how he had done."

I simply couldn't believe that.

"Godfrey is a pro," I objected. "He didn't need reassurance."

"It wasn't that Godfrey needed reassurance," Bruce said. "He knows when he has—or hasn't—done a good show. But it's just that way with all talent, Paul.

There's always that lingering suspicion that the show wasn't as great as they thought."

I sipped my Diet Pepsi and thought about this. It made good sense.

"You're like any other performer in the business," Bruce was saying. "And I'm not putting you on, Paul. What I mean is, to be real talent, a guy has to acquire a certain amount of humility. Otherwise he's a big phony. I figure that talent and humility go together. You're so darned humble at times we should be sponsored by the Humble Oil Company!"

"Watch that, Bruce," I said quickly. "We've got Tresler Comet!"

But inside I was thinking that although the comparison between Arthur Godfrey and me is pleasant to hear, I'm no Arthur Godfrey and I'll never be that big. After I left the Old Vienna that evening, I got to thinking more about what Bruce had said.

And I knew, as I drove home, dead tired, that someday I was going to find this had all been a beautiful dream. What right has a guy like me—with talent so slim it hardly casts a shadow—to be doing a show with people like Bruce and his band? As I drove along, I told myself I'd better cross my fingers and wish on every falling star I saw, to make the dream last. As long as I'm surrounded and helped by Bruce, his band, the girls on the show, the people at the stations, and you—I think the dream may last a little longer, don't you? The Dixon Show may not last but I'll be around for years and years and years.

After all, I'm only thirty-eight.

# 12.

## *Paul Baby &*

# BONNIE LOU

☆ "Is Bonnie Lou actually as rich as you say?"

I wonder if the person who asked me that one day was from the Internal Revenue Service? I'm always kidding Bonnie about being rich. She's the only girl I know who has parlayed a Swiss yodel into visiting privileges at Fort Knox.

But the question stands:

Is Bonnie *that* rich?

Oh, she may not be rich in dollars, but she is rich in about every blessing God has. She is rich in love for people. She is rich in talent. She is rich in warmth, friendliness, and plain old-fashioned decency. So if you get the idea that I think the world of her, lady, you're getting exactly the right idea.

Although Bonnie and I have been together since our morning show began, she can still surprise me with new lines and mixed-up sentences which I love. Also, she can sing more songs off the top of her head than any singer I know. And she knows more big words than a professor—and she has the ability to mispronounce them all. I would be as lost without Bonnie as the King's English is lost *with* her!

When did I first meet this remarkable girl? Well, there I was at WCPO-Radio, spinning records as a disc jockey. One day I looked up and there was Bonnie, outside the control room window, staring at me. She had long, *long* hair, wore a cowgirl outfit, and she had clutched in her hands the record she had made, "Seven Lonely Days." Incidentally that record proved to be one of the many hits that Bonnie has turned out. But then she was just beginning and so was I.

"Mr. Dixon," she said in a shy voice. "If you'd play this record once or twice, that might be the break I need."

I think that was the last time she ever called me "Mr. Dixon."

Anyway, in those days everyone had the mistaken notion that any record I played on the air would be-come—automatically—a hit. But I ask you, how mis-taken can a notion get? You can't put over a record that doesn't have it, can you? As I looked at Bonnie in her cowgirl outfit, I thought the equivalent of: "What's a mother to do!"

I figured the girl was trying to get me to spin a country-and-western tune which wasn't the stuff I played on the air. I had nothing against country-and-western music, but my program wasn't the Boone County Jamboree. It wasn't the New York Philhar-monic, either. Now that I look back, I see that my program wasn't much of anything. I'm surprised I wasn't fired.

Well, I gave her record a "listen." That's disc jockey talk which means I listened to it. Her record was great, it actually was. So, ever since that day, I've been in Bonnie's fan club. That's why when the morning show started on WLW-Television I wanted—and needed—Bonnie on it.

There were problems, though. Bonnie first appeared on our morning show decked out with her long, *long* hair, that cowgirl outfit, lots of fringe, and her cowgirl boots. Bruce and I talked to that girl like Dutch uncles. We finally managed to convince her that the getup she wore looked better on Hayride than it did on our show. She was hard to convince though because she kept arguing back, using long words which she kept mispronouncing.

What *kind* of girl is Bonnie when she's not on camera? Well, she's a doll. Just as she gets involved in long—and complicated—monologues on the air, she gets involved in them when she's not on the air. For instance, one day Gordy, Bonnie, and I were discussing a commercial when out of the blue, Bonnie said: "Oh, I could have bought a mink coat a long time ago, Paul, but it's been a funny thing with me. I never bought one until three months ago. I still don't feel right wearing the crazy thing. Know why? Because people might think I think I'm a little better than they are. And I'm not. And I know it. Paul, when you're in the profession you have got to honor and respect it every hour of every day, don't you? Because, listen, wherever you go—to Kroger or anywhere—you are representing WLW: the people who believe in you.

People have been good to me. I think it's only right that I be good to them. That's how I feel about mink coats. How do you feel about mink coats, Paul?"

Gordon and I looked at Bonnie. We hadn't been talking about mink coats! So we tried to get back to the commercial we had been talking about. We did manage to keep on the subject for two minutes. Then, out of the blue—again!—Bonnie said: "We can't let our hair down too much, can we, Paul? We're always on the stage. So we have to visit and allow time. People want to talk with us. And many times, when we're downtown, they'll stop us on the street and say hello. If we snub them, we're only hurting ourselves. Nobody but ourselves! 'Cause sometimes I don't think we realize how much we mean to these people, I really don't. Isn't that the way you feel, Paul? That's the way I feel. That television tube puts us into their homes every day, lets them know us personally, and gives them the right to have conversations with us when they see us—and no matter how much of a hurry we're in. And we're always rushing, aren't we, Paul?"

Can you see why we love Bonnie!

That girl is as honest as the day is long. She's not affected by the so-called glamor that television stars are supposed to have; and believe me, lady, she *is* a real star. But I'll let you in on a secret: she'll never change from being the girl she is. Just as I came to this Midwest area from Iowa, Bonnie came here from Illinois. She's real people. Ask anyone around the studio. Her mother who was both Swiss and French taught Bonnie to Swiss yodel. Her grandfather was French and her father was German. When Bonnie was born, her birth was an international event.

If it had not been for our Bill McCluskey, this area
would never had been blessed with Bonnie at all. She
was Swiss yodeling on a Kansas City radio station
under the name of Sally Carson. Bill, who happened
to be riding a train from Chicago, sat beside a man
from Kansas City. They got to talking, and Bill mentioned that WLW-Radio was looking for a girl who
could yodel. The stranger, who knew neither Bill *nor*
Bonnie, said: "Well, there's a girl like that yodeling
back home in Kansas City. I don't know her, but I've
heard her on the radio. She's real good."

"When you get back," Bill said, "would you mind
giving her a call and tell her what we're looking for?"

To make a long story short, via a stranger neither
Bonnie nor Bill knew, *that* is how Bonnie came to
WLW!

She adds: "And I've been indebted to that unknown
man ever since. I wish I had gotten his name."

Well, she auditioned for WLW in—of all places!—
Newark, Ohio, because that's where the Hayride was
doing a remote. The station signed her. Bill Mc-
Cluskey himself changed her name from Sally Carson
to Bonnie Lou, and from that moment on, she has
yodeled and mispronounced her way on to fame
in the Midwest via the Hayride and later the Dixon
Show.

"Remember when the Dixon Show first went on the
air?" Bonnie asked me once. "Listen, we sure had lots
of time to kill then, didn't we?"

"That was before the audience got into the act," I
said.

"And before we had many sponsors," Bonnie reminded me.

Lean days or fat days, Bonnie still has the happy

talent of being able to bewilder me. Only the other day when I was doing a commercial for Burger Beer, Bonnie interrupted me to spend five minutes telling about the television drama she had seen the night before on another station. She discussed its plot. She discussed its characters. She rambled on and on. I kept waiting for her to mention Burger Beer. I thought she interrupted me to help with the commercial. But after five minutes, I had the uneasy notion that she had forgotten the Burger Beer commercial completely—which shows, of course, how little I know her. *I* interrupted *her.*

"Bonnie," I said, "what has the television show last night have to do with Burger Beer?"

"But, Paul," she said, "if you'd let me finish, that's what I was trying to tell you. During the commercial on television last night, Milt went to the refrigerator and got himself a Burger Beer."

When Little Joe Cartwright of "Bonanza" came on our show as a guest, Bonnie flipped over him. When I asked why, she raved about his "bedroom eyes." When I asked her what those things were, she said they were eyes that were not quite open.

"But just sort of *half* open—all the time," she explained.

Well, listen, lady, for weeks I went around with my eyes half shut (or half open, I forget which) but that didn't do a thing for Bonnie. All she said was:

"Open your eyes, you idiot!"

I got even with her though. I started a collection of tape recordings of all the bloopers she made every day. Well, almost all of them. I finally had to stop, though. She blooped me out of tape.

But she doesn't bloop *all* the time. That girl—who can croon a sentimental ballad or belt out an up-tempo western tune with equal ease—can pull more commercials out of the fire than her bloops could ever put in. One of her finest hours happened when I was away on a short vacation and Frank Fontaine —"Crazy Guggenham" of the Gleason Show—was doing the Dixon Show for me. A lady demonstrator got stagefright even before she was introduced on camera. When she finally got on camera to do her pitch, things went from bad to worse.

The demonstrator gasped: "I just can't go on!"

"Sure you can," consoled Frank, trying to put her at ease. Since he thought she was going to faint, he reached out to steady her.

*"Get your hands off me!"* the demonstrator quavered.

"Tell us about the product!" Bonnie said quickly. "Honey, what does it do?"

"I'm too nervous to talk," the woman wailed.

"Can I help you?" said Bonnie, trying to keep the show rolling, but she hadn't been briefed on the product, and knew nothing about it. "Honey, which bottle is which? And what do the bottles do?"

Bonnie reached for one of the bottles.

"Don't!" cried the demonstrator. "That makes me nervous, too!"

Bonnie, sensing the commercial and the show and everything else was coming apart at the seams, quickly moved to the Niagara Massage Chair, beamed at the camera, and said: "Why don't we all sit here and relax? It will get rid of that tight and tense feeling. . . ."

A nervous demonstrator? Well, it had to happen somewhere—so where else but the Dixon Show? The payoff? The commercial with the nervous demonstrator attracted more attention and sold more products than had she done her pitch straight. But we'll never convince the demonstrator of that.

And Bonnie isn't alone when it comes to having a flustered demonstrator on tap. Do you remember the problems that *I* had with the one who tried to demonstrate a kitchen slicer in broken English? He had a set pitch. Period. Before he would begin, I would tip off the audience.

"You know, folks," I'd say, "that he's got every word memorized, don't you? If I interrupt him, he'll have to start over—from the beginning."

And *that* is exactly what happened each morning. He would be halfway through his set pitch, I would interrupt, he would look bewildered, and back he would go again—to the beginning—and start over. Sometimes, because I interrupted more than once, the demonstration took ten minutes. A lot of times we went off the air before he could complete it. But was I making fun of him? No. And you know that, don't you, lady? Although the commercial was serious to him—and to me—his pitch was not. Did he mind? Not on your life, lady! As the result of appearing on our show and letting us make hash of his pitch, he sold thousands of slicers he would not have sold otherwise.

But this chapter is about Bonnie. When Bonnie isn't helping with commercials she's either with me at the desk or in the production area singing. I kid her about her music. Once, when she was playing her guitar, I said: "Bonnie, you can't fool me. You don't know a D chord from an A chord."

There's no topping that girl—and some day I'll be smart enough to quit trying because, quick as a wink, she came back with: "Yes I do, Paul. I know there's a difference."

All kidding aside, as a musician Bonnie doesn't have to take a back seat to anyone. She says, she "fools around a little with the violin." Fools around, my foot! She has studied the violin for years. She can still bring down the house—or barn—when she plays her guitar or banjo. Which music—pop or western—does she favor? She says she "likes to do them all." Anyway, she points out, today's music seems to be a mixture of both. Bonnie is right. The line between country and pop is so thin that the difference at times is only the manner in which the tune is presented.

Bonnie feels strongly about music—and friendships. This makes sense because at WLW-Television we're a close-knit family. Ask anyone who works here. I've worked at other stations; each station creates its own mood and its own way of doing things, no one way is right, no one way is wrong, but the relationship between people here at WLW-Television is about as friendly as you'd want a relationship to be. When Bonnie and I were talking about this the other day, she said: "The people here aren't that competitive, Paul. No one is trying to beat the other person or trying to knife him. You just don't find that kind of stuff here. You don't even have that kind of atmosphere. I guess we're trained differently. We're not trained to be one jump ahead of the other guy all the

time. You just do a good job—and you don't have to
worry about being fired in the middle of a show."

She thought a moment, looked serious, and went
on: "Maybe we're a different type of station. Mr. Dunville, Mr. Murphy, and Miss Lyons created this family
type of association. Others who come here from other
stations are surprised to find that we're this way, but
we are. And it shows, doesn't it, Paul? I mean, you
can sense it the minute you walk through the doors."

And want to know something? Bonnie is absolutely
correct!

Anyway, who could ever quarrel with Bonnie about
anything? She's the only girl I know who has served
as a replacement for a tractor pull. No kidding! There
was supposed to be a tractor pull at the Richmond,
Indiana, fair grounds, but something happened. I
think another tractor pull had been scheduled nearby
—or something. So the Richmond tractor pull was
canceled and Bonnie went on in its place!

Bonnie has been with our morning show for nearly
fourteen years—except for vacations and that two-
month interval when she was out because of a nodule
on her vocal chord. We worried about our Bonnie
then. And I was filled with happiness when she came
back to us.

And, when Bonnie's first husband Glenn was killed
in an auto accident, the WLW-Television family ral-
lied like brothers and sisters to comfort her. John
Murphy gave us the company plane so we could fly
with Bonnie to the funeral in Illinois. Marian sang at
the funeral, Bruce played the organ for it, and as for
me—I was proud to walk to the front of the church
between Bonnie and her lovely daughter Connie.

Afterward, when the immediate grief had dimmed, Bonnie endured a string of sad and lonely days. Worse for her was the time each month that tragic day came around again. On that day the poor kid was reliving the tragedy all over again. I didn't have the right words to say, because I'm not the greatest guy with words. All I could say was: "Now, easy, Bonnie. You've got to smile. . . ."

And smile she would—at least, on the show. Maybe she cried all the way home every day, but when that brave girl came on the show each morning for ninety minutes she was a real trooper: she *smiled!* You in the audience helped her. You knew what she was going through. I didn't help pull her through. I can't take the credit. The credit belongs to you. *All* of you.

But even so, it was three months before Bonnie even considered going out on personal appearances. And about that same time, to get her mind off things, she began doing volunteer work at Christ Hospital. She worked there nearly two years before her schedule became so full she had to give up the volunteer work temporarily. What did Bonnie *do* at the hospital? Talked to patients. Delivered mail to them. Ordinary and wonderful things like that. She would go along the corridors, glance discreetly into the various rooms, and if she saw someone gloomy, she'd go in and smile big as life. That's the *real* Bonnie! But if I live to be a thousand, I'll never forget the one day she showed up at the station with tears in her eyes.

"Bonnie," I said. "What's wrong?"

It took her the longest time to tell me, but in halting words, the story came out.

"There was this woman at the hospital," Bonnie

said. "She was passing away. Paul, her mother and father were with her. They said she was struggling to keep alive long enough for her son in the service to get back. She was forty-three years old and she was dying of cancer. I knelt down with her folks and prayed with them. There was nothing else I could do, really, there wasn't. . . ."

Lonely days, but slowly Bonnie was learning to live again.

As she said later, that hospital volunteer work helped her as much, and at times more, than anything else. "It helped me a lot," she said, "to think that at least I was helping someone else. When Glenn left me, I had to look at life different, Paul. I guess I didn't value life before. Now I look at it so different. I cherish every day—every minute—of it. . . ."

And there was that awful time for me when the situation was reversed: *I* was in the hospital and the burden of carrying on the Dixon Show fell on Bonnie's shoulders. Though I may joke about my operation on the show, for a while things were touch and go with me: pneumonia—and a lung operation. Later, in an interview, Bonnie recalled those days: "Each morning was worse than the one before. We never knew whether Paul was going to live until the next day. I would call Marge and all she could say was, 'I—I don't know. . . .' Paul was off the show about three months. We used to give daily reports at first on how he was, but we had to stop giving them. All of the reports were bad. There was nothing good to report, not even a glimmer of hope. They said to me at the station, 'Bonnie, you've got a show to do and you've got to keep the show rolling because Paul will be back. He

*will*, Bonnie, and you've got to believe that.' But believing was hard because Paul was so sick and each
day he got worse. I always put his picture on the desk
during the show. God was good. Paul *did* get better.
And the first day he came back—oh, a tremendous
reaction. After the show I went off into a corner by
myself and bawled. . . ."

And then, happily for Bonnie, along came one of
the nicest guys in the world: Milt!

Shy and unused to the ways of show business, he
was at first bewildered by the world he was meeting.
But Bonnie cheerfully warned him before they were
married: "Now, honey, you're just going to have to
get used to all this!"

He had a lot to get used to, though.

One evening after they were married, he was leaving the station when the Hayride was finished. He
walked through the lobby with Kenny Price—and Milt
was immediately besieged by autograph seekers. Poor
Kenny stood by, looking lost. No one asked him for *his*
autograph and I know exactly how he feels. The same
happens with me when I'm with Scratchy. Anyway,
Milt gave out a couple of autographs but he was confused. He told one of the women: "But why should
you want my autograph? I'm not even *on* the Hayride."

The answer stopped him cold.

"You're Bonnie Lou's husband, aren't you?"

Yes, Milt had a lot to get used to.

When Bonnie first announced her engagement to
Milt—she did it on the Dixon Show, of all places!—
what a day Milt had. He had left his store in Cheviot
to go to lunch. In the meanwhile, three nice old
ladies had been traveling to Cheviot from over the

river. They had to transfer several times to reach
Cheviot, but they were undaunted. They arrived at
Milt's store just after he had gone to lunch. They
trooped in and politely asked where he was. When
they were told he would be gone for an hour, they
plunked themselves down in chairs—and waited.
Eventually Milt returned. The three ladies got up,
walked over to him, looked him up and down, nodded
approval, and said: "Well, we just had to come and
check you out. We don't want Bonnie marrying up
with anybody we don't like."

Milt has yet to get used to the commotion, but he
has come a long way since those hectic days of his
engagement. Last summer at the Ohio State Fair, Milt,
Bonnie, and I were sitting on one of those benches
when autograph seekers came along. Bonnie signed,
Milt signed, and they even asked me to sign. Milt
didn't hesitate. He signed like a real pro. But whose
name did he sign?

Perry Como's!

"As long as I'm in this deep," he shrugged, "I might
as well think big!"

What is Bonnie *really* like? Well, a good example
is how she, Colleen, and Marian get along. To be
honest, you women worry—and scare—me. I never
know how you're going to react. When Colleen joined
the Dixon Show I was a little worried. Bonnie had been
with the show since the beginning and Marian was an
old WLW-Television hand, too. Suppose they resented
Colleen? Well, as you know, it never happened. The
three are like peas in a pod. Later I asked Bonnie
about this and she gave me a look.

"We're all good friends, Colleen, Marian, and I,"

she grinned. "What were you worried about? We couldn't have worked together if we hadn't been friends, but we worked together and were friends, I mean. I showcase her, she showcases me, it's the same with Marian, and honest to goodness, Paul, sometimes I don't understand you at all."

*That* is what Bonnie is like—solid gold.

And this, too, it what Bonnie is like. Each morning before the show starts, I worry about the studio audience. Suppose they don't warm up to me? Suppose they let me die? And when Bonnie is there, I tell her: "Bonnie, I think we're in for a rough one today."

Bonnie will smile and say: "So what? We're lucky and don't ever forget it. They're just like you and me, but God was good to us, Paul. He lets us perform for them. So what we have to do is go out there and try a little harder. That's all."

Try harder? Bonnie could never do that. Each time she's on she knocks herself out completely—and with love.

*That* is Bonnie.

Next question, please.

# 13.

## Paul Baby &

# COLLEEN

☆ "Is Colleen actually as little as she looks on television?" a lady from Maysville asked me. I had met her on the street. Scratchy was with me and she had stopped us for Scratchy's autograph. Then she threw that question at me.

The question is easy to answer. Colleen Sharp *is* as little as she looks—but where everything else is concerned, she's big. Big in talent. Big in beauty. Big in charm. Big in generosity. In fact, lady, she's big so many ways I can't see how she can go through life wearing a size five dress!

What is Colleen like? Well, as Uncle Chris would have said of her: "She's church people."

Which means that she's awfully, awfully nice.

But when we're walking along a windy street together, I worry that the wind might blow her away, or

someone will borrow her thinking she's a souvenir. I
think that is the reason she left Economy, Indiana.
The wind blew her—whoosh!—straight to Dayton
and WLW-D; and finally straight into the hearts of
the Dixon Show audience. Because Dayton is where *I*
found her. She was doing pretty much the same show
we do here: she danced, she sang, she did commercials, she tripped over camera cables, she lighted up
the place with her charm, and she sat behind a desk,
assisting whichever master of ceremonies was running the show at the time. When I say whichever—
meaning there was more than one—I mean what I say
because every time Colleen sneezed, the Dayton program had a different master of ceremonies.

She must have sneezed a lot in Dayton because,
among others, she worked with Doctor IQ, Bobby
Breen, Snooky Lanson, Izzy Kadetz, one of the Ames
Brothers, Vaughn Meader, Dick Curtis, and—finally
—Johnny Gilbert. Then her luck failed. She went to
work with me. I met her first when our Dixon Show
was first going into the three markets beyond Cincinnati. Marian Spelman—and we'll talk about *that*
imp in the next chapter!—and I drove up to Dayton's
WLW-D to promote our entry into Dayton—and
there was this little Colleen—as chipper and as chirpy
as she is today.

Little did I realize as I saw that perky half-pint
trot around the Dayton studios that she would be one
of the keystones of our own Dixon Show. All I knew
then was that she was great, great talent. And also,
she was wearing a pink knit dress that had a ruffle
around the top. Now, why do I remember that!

The reason you all took to Colleen is not compli-

cated. Colleen and you are pretty much alike. She
ain't the eastern high-fashion sophisticate or the un-
washed hippie or whatever those things are. She
doesn't have a phony accent or phony ways. She is the
product of the same Midwest that the rest of us are,
and though she had an opportunity to go to New York,
she turned it down—cold.

No kidding. She took her first real vacation when
she was changing from WLW-D to WLW-Television.
She went with Dayton's Inez Taylor to New York,
to do the town. Naturally, because Inez is an agent,
Colleen tagged along when Inez visited the advertising
agencies. Everywhere Colleen went, she was greeted
with the same story: "Miss Sharp, while you're waiting
for your friend, do you mind reading some lines. . . ."

And there our Colleen would be: taking a quickie
audition. One agency producer told her: "I figured you
were either from Ohio or Indiana. With that accent
you couldn't be from anywhere else. Well, that's what
we find appealing in you, Miss Sharp. We have a
hundred Barbra Streisands walk in here each week.
You know the kind: black eyes, and long hair, and
Bronx accents. But have you noticed the commercials
lately? They are starting to use Midwesterners. If
you'll stay in New York, we can give you more work
than you can use! You've got that well-scrubbed look."

Can you see *now* why the Dixon Show can be considered reasonably successful? I'm surrounded by
talent like Colleen, Bonnie, Marian, and Bruce—all
topnotch professionals! They could easily have made
it big nationally, but they chose to stay here. I'm
glad they made that choice. Without them, our morning show wouldn't last two weeks.

As for Hollywood, Colleen says: "I have no desire

to work there, Paul. First of all, when I was out there I was too busy. Our children were young then. But more important, I know too many girls who went out there and ended up going the wrong route, ending up so ashamed they could never go home. Oh, I know what everyone says: to get a break you have to be in New York or Los Angeles, but I wouldn't have any family life if I did that. . . ."

As for nightclubs, Colleen has this to say: "Maybe television has spoiled me. A television audience in the studio sits there real nice and *listens*. It bothers me in a club, when someone at one of the tables gets loud. I know he has every right to, and anyway, I'm not the kind of person who gets a kick out of putting people like that down. It just hurts my feelings to think that somebody wants to talk while I'm singing."

The *real* Colleen Sharp is still the girl who, along with her sister Barbara, led cheers in Economy, Indiana. In high school Colleen thought about becoming a nurse. But she was already in show business. Along with her sister and parents she traveled and entertained in the three-state area. Think about that. Colleen has been in show business longer than I have been in Cincinnati broadcasting! Actually, when you get down to it, I look upon Colleen as an older sister.

Colleen, I was only kidding! Mercy! Send that Indian of yours back into the teepee.

Gets angry quick, doesn't he?

Oh well, where were we? In Economy, Indiana, watching Colleen lead cheers. Was the high school big? Nope. Colleen's graduating class numbered thirteen! A small town. That's what I told her. But she bristled.

"I wouldn't say that," she muttered. "Besides having

a school, Economy has a post office, two gasoline stations, and a grain elevator. I call that pretty darned big."

The fellow she worked with at WLW-D, on the other hand, had a different name for her hometown. The fellow was Dick Curtis who—to show what a small world this is—discovered that both he and Colleen had relatives in Economy. Not the *same* relatives but you get the idea. And one Thanksgiving, Colleen invited Dick Curtis home for a good old-fashioned Thanksgiving dinner.

"Dick came there," Colleen told me, "and sniffed. Then he said something about certain odors of food cooking that are nostalgic odors. To walk into Economy, he said, was like walking into another world, years ago. He said it was like the Twilight Zone."

The Twilight Zone? Well, that *does* describe Economy where Colleen was raised. The little village on U.S. 35, just north of Richmond, has a homegrown neighborliness like they don't seem to make any more.

And her family feels the same way. Her mother and father, though they now live in Chicago, drive back to Economy every weekend, no matter what the weather is. That's 250 miles each way! They arrive late Friday night, spend the weekend, and on Sunday afternoon, they head back to the Windy City.

"Every weekend?" I asked.

"Well," Colleen hedged. "Maybe not every weekend."

"I didn't think so," I said.

She grinned and said: "They've been in Chicago eight years. At the most, they've only missed a half-dozen weekends back in Economy. So I shouldn't have said every weekend, should I? Daddy is the only man I know who drives 500 miles to cut his front lawn!"

"Say no more," I said. "Economy *is* the Twilight Zone!"

"Don't you want to hear about the house we have there?" she beamed. "It was originally Grandmother's and was a tiny thing at first, but Daddy kept adding on to it. It started out as two rooms, but every time we needed another closet, Daddy would move the toilet, until Mother made him stop. She was afraid if he moved the bathroom any farther from the living room none of us could reach it in time!"

I'll never forget the rainy night Marge and I drove to Dayton to see Colleen perform at a supper club. I had met Colleen briefly before when I was at WLW-D to promote the Dixon Show starting its four-station run. As I told you earlier, I knew the moment I saw her that she was great. And I've told you on the air how I came right back to Cincinnati and told John Murphy that I wanted this girl on my show. So there we were in that jammed supper club.

Later, Colleen told me how she felt about us being in the audience.

"I almost didn't accept that booking," she admitted, "because, Paul, you know how I feel about nightclubs. I'm out of place performing in one. But I figured that with two weeks there, I could pay off this and that, which is how *I* look upon bookings. Well, there I was, doing the second show and out of the corner of my eye, I saw a lot of commotion. I looked over and saw they were moving a table in. Old curiosity got the

best of me, so while I was singing, I looked harder—
and there *you* sat with Marge! I broke out in a cold
sweat. That's how nervous I got. That's when I decided that maybe you really meant what you said
about wanting me in Cincinnati!"

And that, lady, is how Colleen came to Cincinnati,
but she admits she hated to leave Dayton. "Love that
city," she says—and means it. But to Cincinnati she
came—to entertain and to sing.

As for the music she sings on the show, she sticks
close to the standards because, as she confessed to me
once, she knew I liked them. Because she still feels
a little "new" on the Dixon Show (the rest of us have
been on it since the Civil War) Colleen still feels her
way musically.

Colleen has been singing since Hector was a pup.
She started when she was only five—and the first
time she appeared professionally before a live audience was at the Veterans Hospital in Marion, Indiana.
The hospital, part of which was a mental hospital,
scared her at first. She shivered as she recalled her
appearance there.

"It made an impression, Paul, to be that age and
to see those pour souls in the audience with their arms
strapped, just staring at you. I don't think I'll ever
forget that first show! And there was one woman in
another mental hospital in Logansport. She would go
through the year with no makeup of any kind. But
when she heard our little show was coming, she
would get ready weeks in advance, painting her face
with rouge, smearing on gobs of lipstick, and practically burying herself in face powder. And there she
would be in the audience. She would be wearing every

bracelet and piece of jewelry she owned. She made me want to cry because she and all the others were such a warm and responsive audience. . . ."

Colleen and her folks played every kind of booking including—says Colleen—the Swine Banquet in Lebanon, Ohio. Each year her folks premiered their new act at a summer church camp in Remmington, Indiana. Colleen recalls that the first few years the Sharp family opened there, they stayed at a hotel which featured corn-shuck mattresses and a pot under each bed. Later her mother retired from the family act but she still traveled with them. "We called her Wardrobe Mary," Colleen beamed. The first large city that Colleen ever performed in? Cincinnati—at the Hall of Mirrors in the Netherland!

"I was scared to death," said the pride of Economy.

How did Colleen get from the xylophone band to WLW-D in Dayton? Well, Vic Tooker who was a drummer at WLW-D knew the morning show there was looking for a girl vocalist. He had worked with Colleen and her folks on the earlier road shows, so he told Colleen about the job. Mike was then at Ball State College in Muncie, their two kids were babies, and the extra money came in mighty handy.

Colleen likes the idea of doing morning television because as she told Marge one day: "When they first hired me at WLW-D I thought, gee whiz. I mean, wasn't it wonderful to be able to perform and as soon as you were finished for the day, you could be home and with your kids? Other mothers work, don't they? Well, so, gee. I took the job!"

Sometimes women in the audience ask Colleen how many servants she has because they figure with her

workload at WLW-Television she has servants by the
ton. Poor Colleen! The first time she was asked that,
the little kid was floored. She opened her mouth but
didn't know what to say. Servants? Who did they think
she was—some kind of star?

So let's set the record straight. During the school
year, because her children now attend school, no one
runs her home but Colleen. She gets up around 6:45
each morning, wakes the children, and makes sure
Mike is up and about, too. She leaves for the studios
the same time the two children leave for school. And
she is back home before school is out.

"Servants?" Colleen blushed. "Paul, what would I
ever do with one? In Economy we used to clean the
house before the cleaning lady came because we
wanted to make a good impression!"

During the summer, when there is no school to oc-
cupy her children's time, Colleen does get a sitter, for
mornings only. Other than that, she and her Indian
keep their house shipshape and tidy. And no, lady,
they *don't* live in a teepee!

Colleen, Mike, and their children have their big
family days on Saturday and Sunday. Saturday breakfasts are big deals and so are Sunday breakfasts. As
Colleen said: "That's the one time we can all sit down
and get to know one another. The kids look forward
to these breakfasts—and so do Mike and I. These
breakfasts are real events!"

I'm crazy about those two children of hers and they
seem to like me, too, but they don't see the Dixon
Show too often. Well, this figures. During the school
year, they are in school. And in the summer what

kid wants to stay indoors? Once, though, on a school holiday, Colleen came home and asked the two if they had watched us that morning. Shannon looked at Pat, and Pat looked at Shannon.

Finally Shannon had to concede that they had not watched us; they had been watching—of all people!—Uncle Al!

But, if it helps, they felt bad about it. I just hope they will be happy in Dayton with their mother. That's just what I hope. Dumb kids!

Only kidding, Indian. Down, boy, down! Stop dancing around me and stop waving that tomahawk! Besides, the tomahawk says *Made in Japan.* And who ever heard of an Indian wearing a blanket that says "See Seven States from Rock City!" What kind of Indian are you, anyway?

Shannon—"She's eight, going on thirty-two," Colleen mutters—is not impressed with the fact that her mother is in show business. But now and then Shannon will step in to give her mother's career a shot in the arm. For instance, Colleen and Shannon were shoving a shopping cart along an aisle at Kroger and some lady stopped in her tracks and stared at Colleen. You could see what was going through the lady's mind: "Is that Colleen Sharp, the one on television? There she is, big as life, shopping like the rest of us!" At that point, Shannon tugged at the lady's sleeve.

"Yes," said Shannon, the eight-year-old mind-reader. "My mother is *Colleen Sharp!*"

Then Shannon hurried back to the aisle where Colleen stood—and that was that. So let's say her children are impressed as they have every right to be, but

most of the time, Colleen to them is their *mother*—
and *not* "that pretty lady who sings on the Dixon
Show."

And Colleen, herself, shrugs off this business of being in television. She's plain nice people. Everywhere
she goes, though, someone—in a friendly way—is
bound to say: "Where's that Indian?"

"I told Mike," Colleen smiled, "that the minute they
start a fan club for him, he's not coming with me on
any more bookings!"

I will say, though, that in addition to the people of
Economy, Indiana—and frankly, there ain't too many
of them—I am the *only* one who knows how Colleen
got the nickname "Tink." And since this book is going
to tell all, here's how that nickname came to be. Well,
it seems that each afternoon when she was little, her
father . . .

Excuse me a minute. There's an Indian pressing his
Irish nose against my basement window as I dictate
this. He seems angry about something.

I'll be right back.

# 14.

## Paul Baby &

# COLLEEN'S NICKNAME

☆ If you don't mind, lady, I'll tell you how Colleen got the nickname "Tink" in the *next* book I write.

Why?

Because it ain't easy dictating a book when there's a dumb Indian shooting arrows at me.

What I mean is, you run your wagon train, and I'll run mine.

Next question—please. Meanwhile, we'll wait for the cavalry to save the day!

# 15.

## *Paul Baby &*

# MARIAN

☆ "Does Marian Spelman sing the National Anthem every time she turns around?"

How many times I've been asked *that!* As we say, though, when Marian sings the National Anthem she ain't just whistling "Dixie.". Somehow that doesn't sound right, but you know what I mean. What I mean is, she's a lyric soprano—and lyric sopranos can sure sing the National Anthem. They can hit the hard notes right on the button. So, yes. Marian does sing the National Anthem a lot—but not every time she turns around. She sings other things, too.

The thing about Marian that amazed everyone—including Marian herself—is that I wanted her on the Dixon Show. Everyone figured the Dixon Show was not the kind of place that lyric sopranos hang around on. When I asked if Marian could be a part of the Dixon Show, John Murphy himself was surprised.

"She's a great singer," he said to me, "but, Paul, is she right for your audience? A lyric soprano on *your* show?"

"You said the same thing when I asked for Bonnie," I pointed out.

"Bonnie is talented in her own right," John said. "But she's not a lyric soprano."

"No," I said, "what I mean is, when I asked for Bonnie you were surprised because I wanted a girl who was a country singer. But Ruth Lyons proved that Bonnie could do pop stuff as well. And didn't our show prove that there was more to Bonnie than her singing?"

John sighed and gave up. He had a hard enough time trying to explain the Dixon Show to advertisers. He wasn't about to try to explain it to me.

"If you want Marian," he said, "and if she wants to be on your show, you've got her. The next thing you'll be coming in here wanting Bobby Breen," he added sadly.

"Now that you mentioned it, John, I happen to think that Bobby . . ."

I stopped. John Murphy was giving me funny looks. So I left his office—fast. I had won the point. At least, I had Murphy's okay. My next obstacle was Marian herself.

Some obstacles are prettier than others, aren't they? She's one of the prettiest.

Marian was as reluctant as John Murphy was. When I asked her if she'd like to be on the Dixon Show, she peered at me.

"Me?" she said.

I could see what was going through her mind: the Dixon Show needs a lyric soprano like it needs another Oscherwitz salami!

"Your audience is nice," she said, "but, Paul, will they care for the kind of singing *I* do? And another thing, the girls talk with you on your show. I couldn't do that in a million years. And I couldn't make jokes. I just wouldn't fit in. It wouldn't be fair to your viewers."

"They'll love you," I said.

"Are you sure?" she said, still filled with doubt. "Lyric sopranos get funny looks from everybody."

"You see!" I said. "You are a comedienne!"

Well, that blonde came on the show—and you know the rest. She fit in as if she had been there all her life. John Murphy said I brought out a side of Marian the viewers didn't know was there. He keeps giving me credit for this which, however pleasant to hear, is still not where the credit should go. The credit goes to Marian. I couldn't bring out what wasn't in her—and that comedienne in her was there all the time, just waiting for exposure.

There was method in my madness. I knew that with Bonnie on the show, plus Bruce and me, we were attracting and satisfying one segment of the potential audience for the Dixon Show. But I was also aware that out there in "television land" there existed a whole bunch of people the Dixon Show was missing. When Marian came on our show, she attracted *that* segment of the audience—and up went our ratings!

I will admit—and so will Marian—that when she first came on the Dixon Show, she expected to operate strictly as a singer. Bonnie had been the same way, so

I knew what to do. You see, singers—unless they are
on their own shows, as Dinah Shore was—tend to sit
quietly to one side, or wait in the wings, and when
they are introduced, they come out, sing, and immediately sink back into silence again. Marian was this
way, as Bonnie had been.

But I used to kid her when the show was over.

"Marian," I'd say, "let's live it up out there and have
fun."

She is basically a shy girl—which certainly doesn't
show—but that's the truth of her. When I would say
that to her, she would look worried and retreat deeper
into herself. But finally, one happy day, she straight-
ened her shoulders and said: "Well, Paul, I will loosen
up—if you think I can."

From then on, Marian became more than a great
singer; she became a great comedienne, too! It took
courage, but that blonde has the courage. She's great.
So give her the credit. It *all* belongs to her.

Still, she sure sings the National Anthem a lot,
doesn't she? We kid her about it, but her singing the
National Anthem has become as much a part of the
Midwest scene as the Ohio River. She sings it at the
opening game every year for the Cincinnati Reds.

"One year was awful," she grinned. "I was so far
from the band I could hardly hear the music and—
without my glasses—I couldn't see the conductor. So
that year there were *two* National Anthems: the
band's and mine. I don't even know if we started and
ended together. All I know is, we were there on the
same day!"

Marian also sang the National Anthem to open the
New York World's Fair.

She sings it everywhere because by now she feels

it is expected of her. That's why I worry when she and I are on the street. Whenever she sees a crowd, she wants to sing the National Anthem. You should hear her at a crowded bus stop! But I'm only kidding—and both you and Marian know it, don't you? She has yet to sing at a crowded bus stop. She doesn't sing at bus stops because I make her walk down the street wearing blinders!

And did you know that our blonde won the 1951 Metropolitan Opera auditions in Cincinnati!

And did you know that the Corryville flash is a frequent soloist with the Cincinnati Symphony Orchestra in its "pops" concerts?

And did you know that she was one of only four female singers to go overseas with the first "ASCAP Show" on a USO tour in Europe and North Africa in 1955—and that before she left New York Marian sang on the NBC "Tonight" Show?

Well, then, I'll give you a hard one. Did you know that Marian did not even *consider* singing professionally until her son Steve was nearly two years old! Before that, she sang at churches—and that was it!

"My first paying job was singing at a church," she told me once. "I got paid a dollar, but I split that with my accompanist. So I really made only fifty cents!"

Marian came to WLW-Television in June, 1951, as one of the singers on the "Strawhat Matinee" which WLW-T was feeding to the NBC Television network. Ruth Lyons saw her on that show—and before Marian knew what had happened, Marian was working full time here as a staff singer. So if anyone should get the credit for discovering our beautiful blonde, the credit should go where it belongs: to Ruth!

Marian is really many people; she basically reflects

the people she is working with. When she and Shirley Jester get together—that way lies madness! Shirley, one of the nation's finest pianists, has perfect pitch, and has a pixie approach to the world. When she and our Marian entertain, you just sit back and let the wonderful entertainment flow—and hope it goes on forever. When Marian is working with Ginny Blauvelt—the cheerful and happy fashion coordinator— another Marian Spelman appears: the girl who might have made it big on the burlesque circuit as she does her wild impression of fashion models.

When Marian is working with me, another side of her comes out.

What side is that? The comedienne in her! Although she can thrill audiences with an operatic aria, she turns ours on with her wild interpretation of "Diamonds Are a Girl's Best Friend." And she's forever trying to get me out of the basement and upstairs to Marge! Her ways, usually, involve costuming—with my wearing a tigerskin and carrying a club. I have long since stopped trying to top her when it comes to humor. I sometimes wonder what became of that shy blonde who once told me she could never do the Dixon Show.

While the rest of us—Bruce, Bonnie, Colleen, and myself—came from other—and smaller towns— Marian is a product of Cincinnati. She was born and raised in Corryville. When she was in her teens, her family moved to Hyde Park, and that's where she's been ever since. Now she's not there, though. She and Bill Nimmo—her husband—have this farm east of town and the city girl is going wild with farming things.

Yes, the rest of us *are* from small towns. Bruce is

from Ludlow—which is a small and pleasant town directly across the river from Cincinnati. Bob Braun is from Ludlow, too. And three other people.

Marian is quick to point out that although farming is new to her ("My mother didn't even have ferns," she offered) the idea of farming is not new to her husband Bill Nimmo, former network and WLW-T personality who is now with the University of Cincinnati.

"When Bill was a child," Marian said, "he lived on a farm in Westwood—when there *were* farms in Westwood. He used to milk cows and things. And for a dozen years when he was working in New York, he owned a 220-acre farm upstate there."

"What did he raise?" I asked her.

"Cattle—and other crops," the city girl said.

And that is what Marian Spelman is really like!

"Love the smell of barns," she beamed.

And that is what Marian Spelman is really like, too!

# 16.

## *Paul Baby &*

# THE OTHERS

☆ "Now that we know what you're like off camera," a lady from Dayton said to me after a remote, "what about Bob Braun? Is he different off camera?"

"Well," I said. "Bob is—"

"And what about Vivienne Della Chiesa?" the lady went on. "What is she like when—"

"Well," I said. "Bob and Vivienne are actually—"

"And Ruth Lyons," said the lady. "Was she different when—"

"Lady," I said. "Ruth, Vivienne, and Bob are—"

"Then there's Richard King," the lady said. "Is that nut really—"

"Don't you want to ask about Peter Grant?" I said. "And Nick Clooney? And—"

She gave me a look.

"I would," she said. "But you won't let me get a word in edgewise!"

I won't go into the rest of *that* conversation, but she has a point, don't you think? And that is what this chapter is about. It will tell what these WLW-Television professionals are like when the camera is not on them. In other chapters we talked about Bruce, Bonnie, Colleen, and Marian—plus Gordy our producer. In this chapter let's talk about Ruth Lyons, Ruby Wright, Vivienne Della Chiesa, Bob Braun, Peter Grant, Richard King, and—because he's a fixture down here as well as at Columbus—Nick Clooney. I could make this chapter short and say, "Just as nice as they are *on* the air." But I would rather go into details because I'm fond of the whole lot of them, especially Vivienne Della Chiesa which—now that I think about it—is her real name, isn't it?

Oh well, that's what kind of book this is.

First, there's Bob Braun. He kids me and I kid me. I think we're kidding, lady. I ain't about to question it because he's got muscles that won't quit and mine do. Bob? Let's just say that I've known Bob for years. I'm sure that many times he has had the opportunity to leave Cincinnati and go on to what we call in our business the "big time." I'm also sure that Bob has never regretted making his decision to stay in the Midwest. Not that he couldn't have made it. No doubt he would have made it in a big way.

But Bob Braun has also made it in a big way since taking over that fabulous 50-50 Club! He took it over when Ruth Lyons retired and let's face it: those shoes of Ruth were never easy to fill. It took determination, talent, and hard work.

My first glimpse of Bob Braun was on the stage of the old Paramount Theater here in Cincinnati. I was

the master of ceremonies for an amateur show for
Harris Rosedale one night a week. Harris is responsible for giving many kids a boost when they needed it.
Bob was one of the contestants—and if my memory
serves me correctly—Bob won the big event that
night. His prize? A bag of groceries! Yep, even then
he was bringing home the bacon.

Later he came to work at WCPO-TV when I was
there. You might say that Bob and I learned television
together. Later when I came to WLW-T, Bob came
over, too. Only he came via New York where he had
won the Arthur Godfrey Talent Scout Show. From
there to the 50-50 Club—and the rest is history.

The important thing to remember is that success
hasn't changed Bob one bit from the night he appeared in that amateur show at the Paramount. He
still has the same drive, ambition, talent, and hair
that he had then. I guess, at this point, I should talk
about that hair of his. I talk about it all the time on
the air, don't I? Well, his hair *is* nice. I should say that
he wears a rug—I say that on the air—but for the
book, he doesn't. What you see up there on that head
of his belongs to him. Bought and paid for. Oops,
there I go. Only kidding, Bob! Let's get the facts
straight: you *don't* wear a rug! Now, for the love of
Pete, will you put me down!

There! That's *better.* . . .

A strong lad, isn't he? Used to be a lifeguard at
Coney Island. I know because when I went wading
there, he would climb down off the platform and blow
up my waterwings. And say nice things about my rubber swan.

So what is Braun really like? He's just like the guy

you see every day on the tube unless you've got a set
with a very small screen and in that case he's bigger.
Next time you see him, do me a favor, will you? Tell
him I'd like my rubber swan back. Swimming isn't
the same without it!

And then there's Rosemary Kelly who is Braun's
right arm on the 50-50 Club. She comes from a large
family in Price Hill. Her family has so many relatives
scattered about that community that there's a relative
in every block, and she—simply put—is a charmer
and a cutie. Rosie is my kind of people. She used to
be at WCPO-TV, too, when I was there. I think the
reason people just naturally take to Rosie is she can
make friends with a grin, she doesn't put on airs, and
she doesn't try to be pushy—if that's the word I want.
When the camera points to her, she isn't a phony.
Besides, Rosemary doesn't have to pretend to be something she isn't. What she is, is good enough! And you
can see how every day on the 50-50 Club she is in there
trying to add her charming two cents. Richard King
calls her Rosemary Overhang, but that's Richard
King for you. Or at least I think that's Richard King.

I'll tell about Richard King as soon as my druggist
phones in an explanation of him. Meanwhile, let me
answer the question that goes: "What is Nick Clooney
really like?"

Nick used to be here at WLW-T in Cincinnati, but
fate was good to him, he now has his own show in
Columbus, but he's still with WLW-Television.
Couldn't let talent like that get away! Nick Clooney,
although terribly young-looking and quite handsome,
is really old enough to be my father. The Clooney
name is not new to this area, is it? I'm sure you've all

heard his granddaughter, the singer. Rosemary Clooney. Only kidding, Nick—and you know it, too, don't you, lady? But with Nick, you can kid. Some guys you can't. He's quick-witted, sharp as a tack, and friendly as all get-out. When he's not charming his television audience, he's charming everyone he meets —in the studio, on the street, or at the Old Folks Home where he lives.

He has been in business long enough to turn himself into one of the real professionals—but what you see on camera is what you'd see when you meet him in person. He's a guy who is going places and who has earned the right to go as far as he dreams. And our best wishes will always be with him.

Doesn't WLW-Television just seem to collect the nicest kind of people! But thank goodness for Upjohn Unicap Seniors. Nick munches a box a day—otherwise, lady, he couldn't get out of his rocking chair. Ask anyone.

Speaking of potions, I should tell the inside story of Richard King, but be patient. I'm still working on that. In the meanwhile, let's take a look at Vivienne Della Chiesa. Vivienne Della Chiesa sounds like a name you'd see on the side of a Pullman car; you know, *Loch Vivienne Della Chiesa*. But the question we must answer in this chapter is: what is Vivienne really like?

Well, she's new to WLW-Television. This February she celebrated her first year on the air—but she'll be around. She signed a five-year contract! Good news, huh? You bet! I love that girl. She fits in at WLW-Television as if she was born and raised in the control room which—I'll quickly point out—she wasn't.

During the Ohio State Fair in Columbus in 1967 she and I had dinner together almost every evening. I liked the way she never fussed about the check. Without a murmur, she would pick up hers—and mine.

"Never carry more cash than you can afford to lose," I told her. "That's my motto. So I never carry a cent."

Sponsors love her. Her ratings are fabulous. And all that in less than one year here! So take it from there!

Before I tell the true inside story of Richard King, let me say a few kind words about a gentleman who only this year went into partial retirement from the broadcasting scene at WLW-Television. I mean none other than the old "Moon River" announcer himself— Peter Grant. Broadcasting has not been the same since he partially retired. Ruth Lyons tried to marry him off. She couldn't. Neither could the rest of us. Anyway, the secret of Peter Grant is, that long before we got our hands on him, he had already been married. He was married to his true love, broadcasting; and he gives the best that is in him to that affair. His influence is still strong around this place. He gave—and still gives—broadcasting a dignity that it will never quite have again. Pete, you and WLW grew up together. If WLW-Television is big now—and it is—a large measure of its success can be attributed personally to you.

And, lady, Pete has taught us many things. I've never seen him angry—even when things were falling apart. I've yet to hear him say an unkind word about anyone—and some of us deserve unkind words now and then. Pete has encouraged—and still encourages

—every kid who wanders in with stars in his eyes, wanting to be part of broadcasting. Pete was—and is —a darned good newsman. He was—and is—a darned good announcer. Good? Lady, I take that back. He's the best. He can read a telephone book and give that pageful of names so much meaning that you end with a lump in your throat. And nobody but nobody could read the poems the way Pete read them on "Moon River"!

Pete also used to run out to the middle of the street when we had streetcars in Cincinnati. He would grab the motorman's iron from in front of the car, throw the switch in the track, replace the iron, doff his homburg, and run back to the sidewalk. When the trolley cars installed automatic switching devices, the streetcars lost their charm for Pete. But all that is past, isn't it? Pete, who came to WLW-Radio in 1932, has, as I say, semi-retired after thirty-six years of helping us others look better than we were/are.

So goodnight, Pete. But don't expect us to forget you—even though you won't be around as often. Sometimes as I wander the corridors here at WLW-Television I think I hear your voice involved in some amiable discussion. But as I turn the corner, I find that my ears have deceived me. And I miss you—all over again. No, Pete, you may have gone into partial retirement but there's still a large part of you here. So goodnight, Pete. And, as I said, don't expect us to forget you. Nice guys simply aren't that easily forgotten.

And so we come to Richard King who himself has added much to Cincinnati radio broadcasting—a lot of it being medical terms because when Richard doesn't have a known illness he will invent any imaginary one that strikes him as interesting and instructive. A great guy, that Richard King. He has practically changed the pattern of radio disc jockeys all by himself. His programs are so filled with local references that he sounds like the original native of the Queen City. When he is not in front of a microphone he is funny, too. He is so funny, I hate to be around him. They say that other comedians can break Jack Benny up so bad that Benny can hardly talk. Well, I ain't no comedian, but Richard King does the same thing to me. Let him open his mouth—even to yawn—and I start laughing. All he has to do is walk through the corridor, say hello—and I'm in stitches. He doesn't need writers to make him funny. His brain is going all the time. I'll bet he even *dreams* funny.

Who else but Richard King could find a personality like "Usually Jovial" who, when not being Usually Jovial, goes around disguised as mild-mannered Izzy Kadetz of Izzy Kadetz's Kosher Restaurant? And who else but Richard King could engage Art Mehring in so much German language that Mehring's 'copter traffic-reports sound like a foreign broadcast? No, when it comes to being funny, no one can hold a candle to Richard King—and that's a fact! Besides, I have to be nice to him for another reason: Richard King and I have a business going on the side. It's our Home for Wayward Girls. We have our own pickup and delivery system, too. The wayward girls of our home recognize that Richard King is a great comedian the same as I do. One of them said to me only the other day: "There's something funny about Richard King."

So now you know as much about Richard King as the American Medical Association does. They have good reason to be fond of him. He has personally invented more cures than they have illnesses for. And anyone who does that certainly must be all heart. Right?

There's another personality on local television I should tell about. Actually she is not a regular performer in the sense that she gets paid for her work. She's a volunteer. I'm talking about Irma Lazarus who appears regularly on WCET, the Cincinnati educational television station—and every time I turn around she's got me doing another show with her. If we're not standing in front of the Shubert Theater with Mary Martin, freezing and interviewing theatergoers for *this* benefit, we are together in front of the WCET cameras for *that* benefit. Irma is the wife of Fred Lazarus, board chairman of Shillito's. To show what kind of a boss *he* is, the store staff affectionately calls him "Mr. Fred." The Shillito president is a nice guy, too. He's Ross Anderson. I have a great respect for Shillito's for several reasons. One, Marge owes them a lot of money; two, the store once made me Salesman-of-the-Month, an award they usually reserve for Shillito people but they felt I had done a good job on television for them. Nice, huh?

This is taking the long way around, though, to say that it seems impolite for a country boy like me to call the wife of a department store boss by her first name. But Irma Lazarus is that kind of lady. Ten minutes after I first met her, I was calling her by her first name. And I felt right doing it.

What kind of person is she when *she's* not on

camera? She's a great kidder and has a most infectious laugh. I don't think the television cameras do her justice. She's a beautiful creature.

Yes, there are many fine women in television around this area: Irma, Bonnie, Colleen, Rosie, Marian, and—say, you didn't think I'd forget Ruby Wright, did you? She only works the Dixon Show when the other girls are sick or on vacation, but when she does come on, she's the greatest! And every Saturday finds us butterfly-hunting under the covered bridge at Versailles, Indiana.

Some of you asked how the butterfly-hunting thing started. Well, it started by accident, the way the rest of the stuff on the Dixon Show started. Awhile back, WLW-Television put out a memo that it was saluting Versailles for a week and at the end of that week all the WLW-Television stars would appear in a stage show at the high school auditorium there. I read the memo on the air during the Dixon Show. I read the long list of performers who were scheduled to appear: Marian, the Hometowners, Braun, the Lucky Pennies, Bonnie—everybody! As I kept reading I noticed that I had been left off the list and so had Ruby.

"Maybe," I told Bruce on the air, "Ruby and I are mentioned on the next page of the memo."

A voice boomed from the control room: "You idiot, there is no next page!"

I pretended to be hurt.

"Well," I said to the viewers, "Ruby and I don't have to do the show in Versailles, but we'll go anyway. And if we can't do anything else, we'll go out in the woods and hunt butterflies."

We carried on like that for a week. The night of

the Versailles show, the school auditorium was packed. The WLW personnel, using the schoolrooms for dressing rooms, said the kids had written over all the blackboards items like: "We want Paul Baby!"

"Where's Ruby?"

To top the story off, just as the show began, an electrical storm hit the area—and every light in the auditorium went out. The place was pitch dark. Buddy Ross entertained for almost an hour, playing one song right after the other in the darkness. And finally someone in the audience yelled: "You should have invited Dixon and Ruby! They're out there somewhere monkeying with the transformers!"

Versailles, we love you!

Ruby and I both do!

But that's par for the course with Ruby. She loves the world and everybody in it. Barney Rapp is sure a lucky duck. He married that doll! What is she like off camera? As friendly as she is on!

But I have been avoiding one person, haven't I? And I will be honest with you. I rewrote the next part a dozen times, never capturing with words the things I feel in my heart. That's because I'm no writer. So let me go back to the first way I talked it into the dictating machine. Forgive me my errors and my poor writing, but let me say it this way:

Ruth, how can I write about you and what can I say? I thought first of kidding about how "Paul's Pot" helped raise funds for the Christmas Fund. All the women bombarded me with pennies as I sang. But I can't really kid about that. The Christmas Fund is a serious affair. Making jokes just doesn't seem right. So I put that idea aside.

What are you like when the cameras are off? The women of your audience already know, Ruth, because they have always known, haven't they? Wherever you are—at home now or when you were rocking in your chair here at the station—you were the only thing you could ever be: *yourself.* And, Ruth, that's good enough for me and it's good enough for the thousands and thousands of women out there who love you, too.

The thousand and one kindnesses you have shown me flash before me as I talk this. When I was in the hospital, you were there—so *many* times! And you made certain that I wasn't forgotten—and by a thousand little selfless acts, you made me feel better. Yet, to list those acts here would seem impolite, an invasion of the privacy you have rightfully earned. But let me say only this publicly: thank you.

*Thank you!*

Is it true that you're no longer on the air, Ruth? I know it is true but I can't conceive of it. WLW-Television *without* a Ruth Lyons? Impossible. That would be the same as having the sky without stars or the world without love. Ruth, you made this place what it is today. You personally created the friendly atmosphere we now enjoy. Because you were, we can be. I'm saying this badly but you understand, don't you, Ruth?

You've always understood. So how can I presume to say that when the tally lights went off and your show was over for the day, you changed? All I know as I write this is I miss you and that I am not alone. You are missed by everyone.

Do you remember that lonely little ballad called "Have I Stayed Too Long at the Fair?" It tells of a

girl who wanders about the silent fairgrounds after
the clowns have left, the crowds have vanished, and
the ferris wheel has stopped running. I remember one
day one of the girls sang that song on your show. And
I remember that you commented, with a kind of
melancholy, that perhaps you, too, had stayed too long
at the fair. And a few days later, Ruth, you got a letter
that said it better than I could ever have said it. The
letter said simply:

"Miss Lyons, don't worry about *staying too long at
the fair*. Stay as long as you want. Because when you
leave, the fair will be over. . . ."

This book, started so long ago, is done and I am
tired. I will give the last few pages of this to Marge for
her to read. We have been through a lot together. We
have personally lived every page you now hold in your
hand. Great girl, that Marge. And you have been great,
too. All of you, out there in Kneesville. This book may
not set the world on fire, but I've got news for you:
you're the most beautiful bunch of readers that any
book has ever had!

So goodnight, girls.

See you tomorrow on the tube. Don't forget to pull
the shades. Don't let the neighbors in on what you and
I—and all those other beautiful women—have going.

And *thank you* for listening to my book.

# 17.
# And Now
# The LAST Word!!!

by Marge Dixon
—*of course!*

☆ The front door has closed. The big galoot has gone. Greg went with him. And they took the dog Pepper. There Paul and Greg go—the men in my life—for an evening stroll. They do it every night.

And here I sit. I have now read what Paul has written in his book. He came into the living room earlier, handed me the last few pages that represented months of talking into that infernal dictating machine, looked at me sheepishly, and said: "See what you think of it, Marge. I wish I could have made it better, but . . ."

He made a helpless motion.

And now, hours later, I sit here so proud of that

232

guy. So let me borrow that doggone dictating gadget and dictate this chapter to him, may I? Because he needs to be cheered. Men are like that. I guess that is why marriages are so beautiful to women. Our men can go out and do the greatest jobs in the world— climb a mountain, run a lathe, bring home the bacon, cut the grass, or dictate a book—but unless we tell them how wonderful they are, they stumble through life never quite knowing it.

So, Paul, *this* chapter will be from me to you—with no punches pulled. Each of the chapters in your book starts out with a question from someone in your studio audience. It's a bit late for me to start this chapter that way, but let me try the same thing. I've been asked questions, too, Paul. Oodles of them. But they can all be capsuled into one: "How does it feel to be the wife of that 'famous' television personality they call Paul Baby?"

Sometimes that question makes me furious. I mean that, Paul. I know it is asked only in the kindest way and for the nicest reasons, but now and then I get fed up. You see, I'm admitting something that you've known right along. I'm not the most patient girl in the world. But what bothers me is that some people think you're different than other husbands. Honey, if they only knew! How does it feel to be your wife? Are they kidding. How does any wife who is in love with her husband feel?

Doesn't matter *who* you are. If you were President of the United States, truck driver, or garbage man, I would still love you. Come to think of you, you forgot to carry out the garbage this morning, but that isn't the sort of thing I should mention in this book, is it?

By the time this book is published you will have forgotten to cut the grass, get a haircut, fix the lawn furniture, pick up the dry cleaning, and—well, I'll not go on. The list of household chores that you and the rest of the husbands have forgotten to do would fill a book—and all I have is one chapter. So let's get down to cases, Paul.

Namely, *you.*

Right now, as I write this, you and Greg are strolling along the dark streets, talking, I guess—man-things at one another. And here I sit, thinking about the both of you—with love. A *full* life, buster. That's what I'm having, thanks to being married to you. You've come a long way since we met in high school in Iowa. You've had rough times and good times. So have I. There have been events that made you laugh. There have been events that made you cry. But what makes me glow is the thought that in a world filled with doubt, you never once doubted that our marriage was perfect. In other words, darling, you've been great—through the whole ugly mess.

Ooops! Only kidding, Paul. Now you've got me making with the jokes!

A host of memories fill my mind. Seriously, Paul, I mean this. Some of them make me awfully proud. Do you remember when you did the show from Columbus? Governor Rhodes and I came on stage with his two darling grandchildren. I'll never forget how the governor introduced me to that auditorium full of people. He called me gracious and kindly. He said I should be nominated for the Carnegie medal for bravery just for putting up with you. He was joking but he said it with love—the same kind of love that your audiences love you with. You inspire that in people, Paul. You're warm and you're friendly. You make everyone around you want to be warm and friendly, too. Did you know that, honey? Well, now you do. Because of you, the governor said nice things about me. I do wish, though, he had asked you to carry out the garbage. Maybe governors could get husbands to do things that wives can't get them to do.

But I remember other things, Paul. Remember the very first time you did a television remote at WLW-Television? Schott Ford in Newport, wasn't it? You created quite a traffic jam, boy, and all the while you were moaning that no one would show up at all. Art Mehring had to sort out impossible tieups. But what *I* remember about that day was *after* the remote. Do you remember a man came up to you and asked if I was there?

When you pointed me out to him, he came right up to me and whammo! he hit the ceiling. Honey, I'd never seen a man so angry before. And to make matters worse, he was angry at me!

There he stood, practically nose to nose with me, and he was raging: "What do you mean making this man sleep in the basement!!! Don't you know that basements are damp, no matter what kind of home you have!!! Lady, if you . . ."

I'm glad you came by to rescue me, pal. I thought he was going to punch me in the nose.

I must say that being married to you has been interesting. Never a dull moment. At least the girls we meet when you visit other cities know that you're joking about the basement, or do they?

Sometimes I do worry about what you say on the air.

After all, I'm the only wife in the world who ever got an electric petunia cover. And you *know* we have no place outside to plug it in! Anyway, some of those electric things don't work. Remember when I tried to drive nails with the electric hammer? And there you stood, grinning at me.

Men! Ugh! But bless 'em!

'Cause even though you don't carry out the garbage, you've made our house a home. And that's one nice thing that we just have to include in this book. You haven't changed. You're the same Paul Dixon I fell in love with back there in school. Remember? We both used to ride our ponies. Now times have changed, haven't they? Pam and Greg insist on cars. That's all right, though. Where would we keep ponies in the city?

Yes, you're "Paul Baby" to the 150 women who crowd your studio each day. As Mary Wood once wrote in the *Post and Times-Star*, "Paul is the housewives' private pixie, their lovable clown, ageless and fun," but at home you're just another husband. You grumble about high prices. You share the problems we have raising our kids. And you keep asking, "What's for dinner?" Thank God you're human . . . even if you *don't* carry out the garbage.

And we've had our ups and downs, haven't we? We've struggled along as every other couple has, sometimes up to our ears in debt, and sometimes enjoying that rare moment when the first of the month brings only the bills for utilities. Remember when we first came to Cincinnati? We brought along all the mismatched secondhand furniture we owned. Gradually, however, we became a little solvent. So the first thing we did was go out to buy a new couch for the living room. Remember that day, Paul?

We stood around, trying to decide which couch would go best with what we had. It dawned on us that our furniture was so rundown that nothing new would go with the stuff! By the time we left the store, we had bought rugs, tables, lamps, couch, casual chairs, the works—and there we were, walking along Vine Street, both feeling silly as kids, and once more up to our ears in debt!

That's why I think you get along so well with the women in your audience. You know what it is to have to stretch to make ends meet. We stretched for so many years, Paul, we've become experts. Even now I hate to buy new things. I do, though. But those other days aren't so far back there that I can forget them— and I know you don't forget them, either. We've been awfully fortunate, haven't we? We're not rich, but at least we're a little farther along. Haven't served a casserole for—well, for three days.

Some of the stuff you wrote in this book makes me furious at you. Not that all you wrote isn't true, but you wrote the book the same way you do your show, honey. You go around playing yourself down but building everybody else up. They're great. I'll admit that. I love Bruce, Colleen, Bonnie, Marian, Gordy, Mr. Murphy—all of them. They deserve nothing but gold medals because they have to put up with you, too. But, you big idiot—you're pretty good yourself. And don't you ever forget it. I know—because I watch you every day. I wouldn't miss you for the world, pal,

so you'd better get used to that fact. I'm pretty lucky,
you know. What other wife can watch her husband
work? But quit running yourself down so much.

Marty Hogan of the *Enquirer* captured you, Paul,
with words when he wrote: "Maybe it's chemistry.
Maybe Dixon is a kind of substitute husband for the
housewife. Or maybe it's the rapport the guy has with
an audience . . . in a town that doesn't have patience
for phonies."

And why didn't you tell the business side of you in
this book, Paul? I remember the time that Bill Mc-
Cluskey called me aside at a big luncheon in Dayton
and said: "Marge, that husband of yours is the
greatest. Know why?"

"I think so," I said, flattered and pleased for you—
and for me, too. "But tell me."

"Because of the way he is when he's off camera,"
Bill went on. "I've been on a lot of business trips with
him, Marge. And when we get into meetings in New
York, that guy will listen. He's sure of himself, but
there's no braggadocio about him. Inside he's one of
the most humble guys I've ever worked with."

There, you big nut. You put what *you* want in your
chapters—and I'll put what I want in mine!

And in case you don't know what John Murphy
thinks of you, I'll toss that in here for good measure,
too. Once I was standing outside the studio, listening
to you run yourself down on the air, and there stood
John Murphy, listening, too. Well, we got to talking
about you (which is natural; you're my favorite subject!) and *he* said: "That Paul of yours does a good
job of representing Avco, Marge. And that's the truth.
He's a gentleman, well respected, and a good family

man. People like him and have respect for him over and above the fact he's a performer."

I was so pleased, Paul, I almost forgot to put my hand over my heart!

Love that John Murphy!

He sure knows you like a book, but not *this* book, Paul, because you didn't say everything. For instance, John Murphy and I got to talking about the others on the show and how great they are, too.

"Because of Paul," Mr. Murphy said.

When I looked bewildered, he said: "Don't you see, Marge. He showcases them, as Bonnie Lou says. What Paul did with that girl is history. And he found talent in Marian Spelman we didn't know she had—and he had the ability to bring it out. And look what he's done for Colleen Sharp."

Why didn't you include stuff like that in the chapters *you* wrote? Honestly, you make me want to bite nails at times. You act as if you're nothing.

Are your ears burning, Paul Baby? Well, let them burn. If *you* won't say these things in your book, I'll say them in this chapter. After all, this book is about you, isn't it? We want people to see the real *you* as I know you. *You* don't want them to see this side of you, but *I'd* like them to see it. And they know *why* I want to say these nice things. It's because I love you. So there. You and Greg keep walking. I'll keep right on talking into this gadget of yours. Let's see. Now what was it Colleen or Bonnie said about how you mug so much. They were all for it. "Paul has a way with expressions that's terrific," they said. "When somebody else says something he doesn't even have to open his mouth to answer. As a straight man he's great. Actu-

ally, Marge, what we girls say on the show would
mean nothing unless he mugs along with it. He is the
bigger part. Because of that way with mugging, he's
carrying us."

Colleen has developed into a great little mugger
herself, hasn't she, Paul. When I told her this, she
beamed and said: "Well, you must admit there are
times on the show when Paul will say something we
can't very well answer. If we *do* answer, we're going
to get ourselves in too deep. So we just look surprised
or make some kind of face—and let it go at that."

You surround yourself with top talent, Paul. But
why must you keep forgetting that *you* are talent, too?
I know, I know. I can see you shrugging and telling
me otherwise. I can hear you saying: "Now, Marge,
we both know I'm not that good. All I can do is play
it straight with the viewers because housewives can
spot a phony quicker than anyone else in the world.
They know I'm not a singer or a dancer. I'm a mugger,
a hard working mugger, but that's about all. I just love
to laugh, I guess, and I have a ball doing that show.
And the purpose of my show is to make people laugh
and enjoy themselves for ninety minutes."

Okay, have it your way. But you can't fool me.

Even in high school you were the same souped-up
so-and-so you are now. I guess that's why the Albia
High School yearbook tagged you as "The Most Likely
to Succeed." And there was never any doubt about
what you wanted to do in life, was there? You hoped
—even back then—that you were going to make it
big in broadcasting. I remember the time when you
were sixteen that you hurried off to Des Moines to
take an audition. You were certain the radio world

was waiting for you. Your hopes were so high that day, darling. And I remember how you came home crushed. And I can still hear you saying: "The program director said I had a great future—as a druggist."

That was a dark and gloomy day wasn't it, Paul? Remember? We took a long walk—and talked. I can still remember you saying as you took me home: "But, Marge, I'm going to be in radio. You wait and see."

Well, I waited, you big lug, and I've been waiting for you ever since.

After our trip to the altar, you decided to go for broke, didn't you? You wanted to tackle Chicago which was the mecca for the boys with the golden tonsils. Back then it was easy for us to go for broke, pal. We were broke to begin with. I was scared of going to Chicago, but I never told you that, did I? Well, I *was*. And with good reason. I knew we wouldn't starve. But I was scared, Paul. I was afraid you'd have to give up your dream. So there we were: in Chicago.

Trying to conquer Chicago broadcasting was a scary business, remember? Chicago is a big, brassy city with a radio station on every corner—it was the same then—and for every inch of wire holding the stations together there's a glamour boy with damp palms waiting in the lobby, telling himself over and over that he's the best announcer in the world.

What's with Chicago, Paul? Does the wind that whistles in ice cold from the lake intoxicate dreamers like you? Is the wind part of the big time, too?

But you got your job, my glamour boy. Remember the day you bounced into the dinky apartment we had? You radiated. You actually radiated. You were smiling

from ear to ear. You were smiling so hard you could
hardly blurt out the news. WAAF had hired you to do
station breaks! You'd made the "big time"! What a
beautiful moment that was, Paul. At last we were on
our way to making all our dreams come true.

While you were doing your station breaks, I was
peddling pocketbooks in the basement at Marshall
Field and—evenings I created casseroles. Thousands
and thousands of casseroles. Come to think about it,
Paul, you shouldn't complain now about carrying the
garbage out. Back then, we hardly had any at all!
Think *that* over, friend. Anyway, we spent six wild
and wonderful months in Chicago, didn't we? You at
WAAF and me inventing casseroles. You never said
but I know what sometimes you were thinking back
then. You were wishing you had taken the advice of
that Des Moines program director—and gone into
pharmacy! The beautiful dream was getting a little
frayed about then, wasn't it? But as they say, you
"hung in there," and finally the trail led to Cincinnati.

That was twenty wonderful years ago and at the
time we wondered how long we would last. First you
did the newscasts. Then you were a disc jockey. And
finally along came television where you really hit it
big. You and television just seemed made for each
other!

Then, Paul, NEW YORK CITY!!! Even now I think
of that city in terms of capital letters. Remember how
excited we were? If Chicago was big time, New York
was bigger. Yes, darling, our hopes were high but why
were our hearts so sad? I knew but never said; and so
did you. We had come to love Cincinnati and this
Midwest area a little too much. Iowa was behind us.

Chicago was behind us. But Cincinnati was where you had found the right niche. You loved the people— and they loved you back.

To leave Cincinnati and our friends? Our hearts were sad but we never said. I encouraged you, you encouraged me. We each thought New York was what the other wanted. Why are married people that way, Paul? We know one another as well as two people ever will know one another. Yet, just as other husbands and wives do, we each play little games of pretend for the sake of the other. And so there we were, in New York!!! It was a sorry game, wasn't it?

Oh, sure. I was proud of you because you had made what people called the big time. You had earned the right to it. And you knocked yourself out there, too. You never do things halfway. Only along came John Murphy. Remember the night we three had dinner together? You wrote of it in the chapter about John, but you only touched upon it. I suppose men aren't allowed to admit that they can get lonely and home- sick, too. I was so lonely for Ohio—and our friends in Cincinnati—after John left us that evening I wanted to cry.

I'm not talking about our personal friends and neighbors. They were a part of my loneliness. But so were all the other friends—the unseen and wonderful people who flooded my hospital room with cards and letters and presents when Pam and Greg were born. These were your listeners and viewers, Paul, but I always think of them as my friends, too. Is that all right? I hope so. Well, Paul, I was lonely for them, too. New York may be great but give me a streetful of Midwesterners any old day!

That shows what kind of girl you married, honey. I'm just not the glamorous type. Okay? And let me add one more note here about New York. Paul, I've never told you this before but I think one of the bravest things you ever did was kiss New York goodby and kiss the Midwest hello again. Remember how our New York friends were shocked at the choice? To them, I guess, the world is flat. They couldn't conceive of anything beyond the Hudson River. New York and its suburban areas were all they knew. Go west of the Allegheny Mountains? Heavens! They'd never do that. They would fall off! I'll never forget you in the living room, telling our New York neighbor: "I meant what I said in my letter of resignation. My wife and my kids come first. I want them to be happy. I admit I still have a taste for New York and I loved working here. But I hated living here. Don't you see? I guess that proves what I should have known all along: I'm just a country boy at heart."

Are you kidding, Paul? To me that evening in the living room you stood so tall! And now you and Greg are out for a walk, walking the quiet streets of our Cincinnati neighborhood. Greg is as tall as you are now. Do you realize that? Tonight a man and boy aren't taking a walk. Two *men* are. And I sit here at home, thinking again of that New York decision, and falling in love with you all over again which, pal, you must admit is hard to do.

I'm botching this chapter up, aren't I? I pretend to be so organized and I'm really not. First I blurt out this and then I blurt out that. All I want to do is let your viewers see the side of you that you would rather keep to yourself. I think they *do* see it—even without my telling them. But you owe this much to them, Paul. And you know it, too. We owe a lot to the people who help you. That includes the audience as well as all the people behind the scenes. You're lucky when you think about it. Each weekday 150 good friends come to call on you!

And *I'm* lucky. Suppose they dropped into the house each day? They'd be welcome, but think of the coffee-cups I'd be washing! Whew! Tell them hello for me, give them my best, but please: *don't* invite them over for lunch! Work your magic on them at the station, honey.

Frankly, although I know you like a book—say, that's a joke, isn't it!—I still can't figure out *what* it is that you *do* on your show each day that works the magic. I don't know how you weave it, but weave it you do: in the Cincinnati, Dayton, Columbus, and Indianapolis areas. And in our home, too. Ratings say that your show attracts more women viewers than watch the nine competing channels combined.

Why? Well, Paul, I guess the people see in you what I see in you. They see a big hunk of man who will gladly help a girl off her horse but who sometimes needs to be reminded to come in out of the rain. They see a rather wonderful guy who kids his audience, the performers on his show, his producer, but who never fails to kid himself. They see a guy who is able to cope with the pressures of a daily 90-minute television pro-gram simply because he talks from his heart.

And I've seen other sides of you, Paul. In my mind I have a private picture collection of mental snapshots that I have taken of you. One shows you standing dumbfounded with joy right in the middle of our kitchen—when I told you we were going to have our first baby. Another snapshot shows you standing dumbfounded with joy *again* right in the middle of our kitchen *again* when I told you we were going to have a baby *again*. I will admit that for several years after Greg was born you seemed reluctant for me to say anything in the kitchen, but that's life.

I have so many mental snapshots of you, Paul. One shows you in the living room. You should have seen the wonder in your eyes as you watched Pam take her first steps. And I have a snapshot of you coming into my hospital room when Greg was born. I have a picture of you when Pam went to school the first day. I have a picture of you, honey, when you were sick. I'm sorry I can't make that picture go away. You were so sick, Paul, and we were so afraid.

You will be home soon, won't you? You and Greg. The two men in my life. Well, I've read your book. I like it. And I hope the publisher will let me add this chapter, *as is*, because I think it tells about you in a way that you could never tell about yourself. And it tells about you in a way you won't let the others —Bonnie, Colleen, Marian, Bruce, and the rest—tell about you on the air. So you hurry home.

They may need you at the station, but you've a girl here—two of them, in fact—who need and love you, too. And I guess *that* answers the question of how it feels to be the wife of the famous (?) television personality they call Paul Dixon! What I mean is, in a day filled with television, advertising agencies, sponsors, ratings, and three children—one of which is cleverly disguised as a husband—you don't feel, folks, you just don't feel!

So hurry home, Paul. There are two things I'd like you to do.

The first is carry out the garbage.

# About the Author

☆ PAUL BABY is, in part anyway, an autobiography of Paul Dixon—and if you are within television range of WLW-TV in Cincinnati, Dayton, and Columbus in Ohio, and Indianapolis in Indiana, we need say no more. Nearly everybody in four states knows who that rascal is.

If you're the exception—and *don't* know—we can explain him best by saying he's the nice guy down the street, and at your last party he told jokes, wore lampshades, got sentimental over your baby, and got serious over the way the world is. In other words, he's a regular outgoing guy, full of good will, and is as comfortable as an old shoe. The difference is, he is himself not in your living room but on television—five mornings a week, 90 minutes a morning. His neighbors swear by him—and his neighbors, via the tube, are legion.

Paul Dixon is no doubt the most popular TV personality in the Midwest. The "regulars" on his program—singers as well as the prop boy—are well-known in a million homes, too. Paul's enthusiastic ad-lib commercials, the astonishing contributions of the ladies in the audience, his wacky clowning, his goofs, his utter disregard for trying to be a Hollywood master of ceremonies—well, this is Dixon and this is television at its finest.

Iowa-bred, the son of a small-town druggist, Paul Dixon came up through the ranks of radio and then television in Des Moines, Chicago, New York, finally becoming MC of his own extraordinary show originating in Cincinnati.

His early recollections of radio (do you remember Fibber McGee's closet or Bulldog Drummond coming "out of the fog . . . out of the night?") are as entertaining as his daily misadventures on TV (read all about the lady who brought her exotic bathroom-tissue collection to the studio).

Does this book tell *all*? Mercy, as Dixon would say. Where Dixon is concerned, who knows what *all* is? He says he can't sing (he can't), he says he can't dance (he can't), and he says he can't tell a joke without messing up the punch line (and he can't). What *can* he do?

Well, he can make thousands upon thousands of women spend 90 minutes with him each morning. And each day that number grows larger! Yep, each morning those ladies are there—and loving every minute of it. This book tells why. Or, we think it does.